Sul GOAL

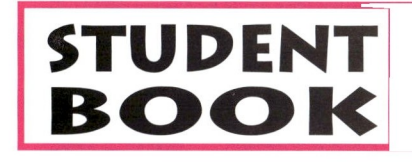

STUDENT BOOK

Manuel dos Santos

Boston   Burr Ridge, IL   Dubuque, IA   Madison, WI   New York   San Francisco   St. Louis
Bangkok   Bogotá   Caracas   Kuala Lumpur   Lisbon   London   Madrid   Mexico City
Milan   Montreal   New Delhi   Santiago   Seoul   Singapore   Sydney   Taipei   Toronto

Editorial Director:	Tina Carver
Senior Managing Editor:	Louis Carrillo
Development Editors:	Janet Battiste
Wordplayers:	Jacqueline Flamm, Dina Forbes
Art and Design Director:	Heloisa Tiburtius
Book Design:	Heloisa Tiburtius
Electronic and Design Production:	Amaryllis Kanayama, Edu Moreira
Cover Design and Production:	Heloisa and Osmarco
Illustrators:	Carlos Zubek, Daniel Cabral, Edson Kohatsu, Edu Moreira, Fábio Belem, Frank Maciel, Jairo dos Santos, Luri Kohatsu, Rodrigo Borges, Rogério Coelho, Tiburcio

Photo Researcher: Rachel Martin
Photo Credits
Cover: © Corbis; 8: © The Mariners' Museum/Corbis; 9: © Corbis; 10 © Stockbyte (top); © Philip Coblentz/Painet (middle); © Greg Girard, 1992/PictureQuest (bottom); 11 © Janis Christie/Photo Disc (top); © Michael Freeman/Weststock (bottom); 18: © Rykoff Collection/Corbis; 21: © PRNewsFoto/Compaq Computer (top left); © Siede Preis/PhotoDisc (top middle); © Corbis (top right); © PRNewsFoto/Sensory Science (bottom left); © Tomas del Amo/Weststock (bottom middle); © PRNewsFoto/Magazine-of-the-Month Club (bottom right); 22: © Ellis Herwig/Picture Quest; 24: © AP Photo; 26: © Earl & Nazima Kowall/Corbis (top); © CMCD PhotoDisc/Picture Quest (middle); © Painet (bottom); 27 © Eric Meola/The Image Bank (top); © AP Photo/John Miller (bottom); 29: © AP Photo/Adil Bradlow (left); © Ryan McVay/PhotoDisc/PictureQuest (middle); © AP Photo/Nick Ut (right); 37: © Bettmann/Corbis; 82: © John Laptad/Weststock (top); © AP Photo/Roberta Bore (bottom); 83: © Brian Drake/Weststock; 84: © Don Tremain/Photo Disc/Picture Quest; 85: © Corbis; © Don Tremain/Photo Disc/Picture Quest; © eyewire; 93: © AP Photo/Michel Lipchitz; 113: © Robert Holmes/Corbis (middle); © Bettmann/Corbis (top right & bottom right)

When I'm Sixty-Four
By: John Lennon and Paul McCartney
Copyright © 1967 Sony/ATV Tunes LLC. (Renewed) All rights
administered by Sony/ATV Music Publishing, 8 Music Square West, Nashville,
TN 37203. All rights reserved. Used by permission.

SuperGoal 4
1st Edition
Student Book

No part of this publication may be reproduced or distributed in any form or by any means, or stored in a data base or retrieval system, without the prior permission of the publisher.

Copyright © 2001
The McGraw-Hill Companies

ISBN
970-10-3342-6

Printed in Singapore

Contents

SCOPE AND SEQUENCE — iv

1. BACKGROUNDS — 2
2. CAREERS — 10
3. WHAT WILL BE WILL BE — 18

EXPANSION 1 — 26

4. ONLY THE BEST — 30
5. DID YOU HURT YOURSELF? — 38
6. TAKE MY ADVICE — 46

EXPANSION 2 — 54

7. DEAR FRIENDS — 58
8. WISHFUL THINKING — 66
9. COMPLAINTS, COMPLAINTS — 74

EXPANSION 3 — 82

10. I WONDER WHAT HAPPENED — 86
11. IF I'D ONLY KNOWN — 94
12. WHAT THEY SAID — 102

EXPANSION 4 — 110

VOCABULARY — 114

Scope and Sequence

UNIT TITLE	FUNCTIONS	GRAMMAR
1 BACKGROUNDS Pages 2-9	Talk about personal features and personality Talk about one's relatives Talk about immigrating and adjusting to a new country	Simple present tense Simple present vs. present progressive Simple past tense Adverbs of degree: *a bit/a little, extremely, not at all, quite, rather, somewhat, really, very*
2 CAREERS Pages 10-17	Talk about how long one has been doing something Talk about careers Talk about job applications	Present perfect progressive tense: affirmative, questions, short answers Adjective + preposition + gerund
3 WHAT WILL BE WILL BE Pages 18-25	Make predictions about the future Express opinions Make arrangements	Future with *will* or *going to*: affirmative, negative, questions *Will* vs. *be going to* Future progressive tense: affirmative, questions The present after *when*
4 ONLY THE BEST Pages 30-37	Talk about commercials, ads, and product history Describe products Make comparisons	The passive Comparatives and superlatives Verbs *look, smell, sound, taste* with *like* + noun
5 DID YOU HURT YOURSELF? Pages 38-45	Talk about accidents Talk about cause and effect	Reflexive pronouns *Because* vs. *so* *If* vs. *in case* *So* and *neither* Verb + gerund or infinitive
6 TAKE MY ADVICE Pages 46-53	Discuss common problems Ask for and give advice	Modals: *should, ought to, might, could* *Had better* Two- and three-word verbs Infinitive of purpose: *in order to* *So* and *therefore*

LISTENING AND PRONUNCIATION	READING AND WRITING	LEARNING STRATEGIES AND SKILLS*
Listening: listen for information in a conversation Pronunciation: emphasis on important words in sentences	Read about immigration in the United States Write about oneself and one's family Write about people who have moved from one country to another (Project)	Look at the title, pictures, and first and last paragraphs of a reading to predict the topic Make comparisons
Listening: listen first for general understanding and then for specific information Pronunciation: /m/ /n/ /ŋ/	Read ads for internships Read a résumé Write a letter of application Write a résumé	Predict a topic based on a title
Listening: listen for information to fill in a chart Pronunciation: Unstressed words in sentences	Read lyrics of a song Write about music that will be popular in the future	Find rhyming words in a song Form opinions
Listening: write key words while listening Pronunciation: Word stress for emphasis and/or exaggeration	Read about the history of a popular food Write about the history of a product Write an advertisement for a product	Make comparisons to understand a reading Analyze paragraphs individually to understand a reading Summarize to facilitate memorization Look for key words
Listening: know information to listen for Pronunciation: final consonant clusters	Read about unusual accidents Write about an accident one had or witnessed Write a safety campaign (Project)	Use pictures to predict a topic Read subheadings to understand changes in topics
Listening: listen for key words Pronunciation: Stress in two-word verbs	Read about ending relationships Write advice about a common problem Write about community resources (Project)	Scan for information List ideas about a topic before reading

UNIT TITLE	FUNCTIONS	GRAMMAR
7 DEAR FRIENDS Pages 58-65	Make and accept an apology Accept and refuse an invitation Give excuses Make arrangements	Preposition + gerund Adjectives followed by prepositions Future in the past *Although* vs. *in spite of* Adverbs of degree: *so . . . that* *Can–could* Clauses of time: *as soon* and *when*
8 WISHFUL THINKING Pages 66-73	Talk about hypothetical situations Talk about probability or improbability Talk about predicaments Give advice Wish for something	Second conditional: *If I had . . . , I would . . .* Contractions with *would* Conditional with *could* and *might* Verb *wish*
9 COMPLAINTS, COMPLAINTS Pages 74-81	Talk about what needs to be done Ask to have something done Talk about common consumer complaints Discuss consumer awareness and rights	*Need to be done* *Get/Have something done* Past participles as adjectives
10 I WONDER WHAT HAPPENED Pages 86-93	Talk about events that happened in the past before others Speculate about facts	Past perfect tense: affirmative, questions, short answers *Can't be/might be/must + be* *Should have* + past participle *Whatever, whoever, whenever, wherever*
11 IF I'D ONLY KNOWN Pages 94-101	Talk about missed opportunities Talk about regrets	*Should have* + past participle Third conditional: *if* + past perfect + *would* *If* with *could* and *might*
12 WHAT THEY SAID Pages 102-109	Report what people said Discuss famous quotes Relate messages	Direct to reported speech: statements and questions, word changes in reported speech

LISTENING AND PRONUNCIATION	READING AND WRITING	LEARNING STRATEGIES AND SKILLS*
Listening: listen for vocal cues in telephone messages Pronunciation: /ɛ/ /æ/ /ɪ/	Read about the history of communication Write an excuse (note to teacher, school excuse) Write a letter giving good or bad news Write greeting cards (Project)	Identify examples in a reading Use language to assess the formality of a situation
Listening: listen for specific information Pronunciation: reduction of *would you* and *could you* in Wh- questions	Read about Robinson Crusoe Write about a survival story or adventure story	Use familiar words to understand new vocabulary Use the introduction of a reading to predict language
Listening: take notes while listening Pronunciation: sounds of the letter *u* /uw/ /ʊ/ /ə/	Read about bad luck Write a letter of complaint about a faulty product Write advice to consumers about a complaint	Relate personal experience to examples in a reading
Listening: listen for general understanding Pronunciation: final /ər/	Read about meteors Write about an unusual occurrence or discovery	Speculate about a topic Use pictures to assess a situation
Listening: listen for specific information to fill in a chart Pronunciation: reduction of *could have*, *should have*, and *would have*	Read an advice column Write advice	Use clues to determine verb tense
Listening: listen for verbal cues to understand meaning Pronunciation: letter combination *ou* /ə/ /uw/ /aw/	Read some famous quotations Write a phone conversation Write about interesting quotations	Understand irony in a reading

* The strategies and skills in this column are in the Student Book.
   For additional ones to present, see the Unit Goals in the Teacher's Manual.

1 BACKGROUNDS

LOOK AND LISTEN

"United Players"
present

William Shakespeare's

ROMEO & JULIET

Opens July 10
at the Circle Theater

About the Players
The members of this amateur theater group all come from different cultural and ethnic backgrounds. But they all have one thing in common—their love for the theater.

Amanda Johnson was born in New Orleans, of African-American parents. Her native language is English, but she's majoring in French and Italian. She is tall and dark with curly hair. She has a very outgoing personality. Amanda acts and directs.

Andy Rodriguez is Cuban American. His parents immigrated to the United States in 1982, and Andy was born in Miami. Andy is dark, good-looking, and extremely talkative. He is fluent in English and Spanish. Andy dances very well, and he can play several instruments. Andy is working on a business degree.

Carol O'Neil is of Irish descent. She was born in Chicago. Carol works as a waitress during the day, and she is studying dramatic arts at night. She has red hair, grayish-green eyes, and freckles, and she is quite slim. Carol has a strong personality, and she is the group's public relations person. She can play the piano and keyboard, and she has a wonderful voice.

Van Thang was born in Vietnam, but his family moved to the United States when he was seven years old. Van's native language is Vietnamese, but he feels he can express himself better in English. Van has somewhat long black hair, he's of average height, and he's a little reserved. He lives in a dorm, and he's majoring in engineering. This is Van's first public appearance, and he's rather worried about his performance.

Sacha Ustinov came to the United States five years ago, and he still speaks English with a bit of an accent. His native language is Russian, but he is also fluent in German. Sacha has fair hair and light skin, and he looks younger than he actually is. He is very sociable and makes friends easily. Sacha is studying architecture.

1 COMPREHENSION

Complete the chart about each person in the group.

Name	Language(s)	Ethnic background	Appearance/Personality

2 PAIR WORK

Ask and answer about the people in the play.

A
- Where was <u>Andy</u> born?
- <u>He was born in Miami.</u>

- What languages does <u>Van</u> speak?.
- <u>He speaks Vietnamese and English.</u>

- What is <u>Amanda</u> like?
- <u>She's tall, dark, and she has curly hair.
She has an outgoing personality.</u>

- What is <u>Sacha</u> studying?
- <u>He's studying architecture.</u>

B Write down basic information about yourself, and exchange it with your partner.

3 GRAMMAR

Simple present tense

Use the simple present tense to give facts and to talk about habits or routines.

A: Where **are** you from?
B: I**'m** from Hong Kong.

A: Where **do** you **live**?
B: I **live** with my relatives in L.A.

A: What **does** your father **do**?
B: He**'s** a university professor.

A: What **does** he **teach**?
B: He **teaches** social science.

Simple present vs. present progressive

Temporary   Permanent

Chen **is staying** with her aunt in L.A., but she **lives** in Hong Kong.

Note:
Verbs of feeling and opinion are not normally used in the progressive: *believe, doubt, feel, forget, hate, hear, know, like, look, love, remember, see, seem, think, understand.*

We say: I **like** plays. **NOT** I**'m liking** plays.

Note:
The present progressive can also describe actions true for the present but not actually occurring at the moment: *Jane's studying French at the university.*

Simple past tense

Use the simple past to talk about events that began and ended in the past.

I **grew up** in Florida. We **moved** to California last year.

Adverbs of degree

Use adverbs of degree to change the strength of adjectives.

not at all   a bit/a little   rather   somewhat   quite   really   very   extremely

The performance was**n't at all** interesting.

A Complete the sentences. Use the simple present or the present progressive.

1. The people in the audience ____aren't clapping____ (not clap).
   I don't think they _____ (like) the show.
2. Jack _____ (believe) that I was born in the United States because
   I _____ (have) a good American accent.
3. The actor _____ (not understand) some of the lines in the play.
   The director _____ (explain) them to him now during the rehearsal.
4. The actors _____ (rehearse) the play on the stage now.
   They _____ (seem) a little nervous.

4

B Complete the sentences. Use the correct adverb of degree. More than one answer is possible. Compare your answers with a partner.

1. He's _____ late.
2. They're _____ late.
3. It's _____ funny.
4. It's _____ early for lunch.
5. She's _____ sleepy.
6. They're _____ tired.

C Complete the letter with the correct forms of the verbs. Use simple past, simple present, or present progressive.

Dear Mario,

How is it going? I hope you are well and that you _____ (not work) too hard.
College life in the United States _____ (be) very different from the way it is at home. Students _____ (send) applications to colleges all over the country, and they may go to a school hundreds of miles away from their home. Most college campuses _____ (have) dormitories. But often students _____ (find) their own accommodations off campus. I _____ (be) lucky when I _____ (arrive). I _____ (get) a nice comfortable room in a dorm. I _____ (share) it with a student from Ghana.

It _____ (be) winter here now, my first winter in the United States. There _____ (be) snow everywhere, ten feet deep in some places. I _____ (learn) to ice-skate, while you _____ (swim) in the warm ocean. When I _____ (apply) for this scholarship, I _____ (know) it _____ (be) a great opportunity, and I _____ (want) the experience of living abroad. I really _____ (like) this country, but I _____ (miss) you all, and sometimes I _____ (feel) really homesick.

I must go now. My friends _____ (call) me for the rehearsal. Yes, I _____ (be) a member of the drama society, and I _____ (take) acting classes. Maybe I'll end up in Hollywood, after I complete my studies in engineering.

Best regards,

Daniel

5

4 GRAMMAR TALK

A Find out the following information about your partner. Then introduce him/her to the class.

1. Full name
2. Where he/she lives
3. Where the person was born
4. Where he/she grew up
5. About his/her family background
6. What the person likes or is interested in
7. What the person doesn't like
8. Your idea: _____

Example:
I'd like to introduce Mei Li. Mei means "pretty" in Chinese. In China, people put the family name first and the given name second. Both names are used, so Mei Li's full name is Wang Mei Li. Mei Li was born in Beijing, but she grew up in Shanghai. Her father . . .

B Discuss in groups who in your class should get the parts in the play *Romeo and Juliet*. Tell why.

5 LISTENING

A Listen to the conversation between Tony and Monica. Answer the questions.

1. Where are the two people?
2. What do they have in common?

B Listen to the conversation again. Answer the questions.

1. What problem did Monica have with the lecture?
2. Where is she going now? What for?
3. What are Monica and Tony majoring in?
4. Where is Monica from?
5. What is an extremely interesting coincidence in the conversation?

6 PRONUNCIATION

Listen and practice. In English, speakers can stress or emphasize words they think are important. Usually, however, these are content words like nouns, verbs, and adjectives.

What are you **doing** after **class**?	They're **waiting** for the next **act**.
What **seats** did you **get** for the **show**?	**Marie** was **born** in **France**.
Did you **like** it?	The **actors** are **learning** their **lines**.

7 CHAT TIME

1. Where is your family from?
   Did people in your family ever move to, or live in, a different country?
2. Do you have relatives in other cities or countries? Have you ever visited them?
3. Are there many immigrants where you live? Where do they come from?
4. Do many people immigrate from countries you know? If so, why do they immigrate?

8 — CONVERSATION

Luisa: Tell me about yourself.
Chen: I was born in L.A., but my family is from China. My father came to the U.S. to study. He got a Ph.D. in computer science, and he stayed on as a professor at a college in California.
Luisa: Is your mother from China, too?
Chen: No, my Mom is from here. She's Asian American. Her folks came to the U.S. during the nineteenth century. In fact, one of her great-grandfathers actually helped to build the first railroad across the United States in the 1860s. What about you?
Luisa: Well, I'm a third-generation Mexican American. My grandparents were born in Veracruz, and they immigrated to this country a long time ago. We still have a lot of relatives in Mexico.
Chen: Do you keep in touch with them?
Luisa: We visit whenever we can.
Chen: Well, I'm afraid we've lost touch with my father's family. By the way, how's your Spanish?
Luisa: It's pretty good. We speak it at home most of the time. Do you speak Chinese?
Chen: Yeah, I'm quite fluent, but I can't write it.

ABOUT THE CONVERSATION
1. Where is Chen's family from?
2. What does his father do?
3. Does Luisa still have family in Mexico?
4. Does Chen visit his family in China?
5. What is Luisa's native language?
6. Can Chen write Chinese?

9 — YOUR TURN

A Role-play and give information about your families. Use the following prompts to ask questions.

> where/born
> where/parents or grandparents born
> what languages/parents or grandparents/speak
> what/parents or grandparents/do

B Do the following role play: You haven't seen an old friend for a long time. Tell him/her what you and your family members are doing.

READING

BEFORE READING
What do you think the reading is about?

> **READING**
> Before you read, look at the title, any pictures, and the first and last paragraphs. This gives you an idea of what the reading is about. Then think about what you know about the topic.

THE UNITED STATES: A NATION OF MANY NATIONS

Between 1880 and 1920, 23 million immigrants arrived in the United States. Most of them came from poor towns and villages in southern and eastern Europe. They had one thing in common. They believed that in the United States, life was going to be better for them. It was the land of freedom and prosperity.

Most of these immigrants were able to get just enough money to pay for the trip across the ocean by boat. Many arrived without any money to their names. Often the father of a family came first and found work. Then he sent for his wife and children.

The trip for poor immigrants was terrible. Men, women, and children stayed in crowded and smelly compartments, deep down in the hold of the ship. They had no showers. There were no dining rooms for them. They went up on deck to get food from huge pots. This was the price they had to pay to get to the "New World."

Here is one immigrant's memory of his arrival in the United States from Italy at the age of nine: "I'll never forget my first impressions of America. The deck was full of passengers, and I stood there, eyes wide open, holding my mother's hand, while my father lifted my baby sister to see the Statue of Liberty."

They saw the Statue of Liberty in New York Harbor, but they weren't free to enter America right away. When immigrants landed in New York, ferryboats took them to Ellis Island.

At Ellis Island, immigration officers questioned new arrivals, and a doctor examined them. Those who failed the medical exam had to go back to their country. Sometimes if a child was ill, the entire family had to return. Ellis Island became known as Heartbreak Island among immigrants.

Life was hard at first for many immigrants, who worked long hours for low pay. They did not find the streets paved with gold. Many lived in overcrowded buildings in the poor sections of large cities. But often their children managed to have more prosperous lives.

Today, more than 40 percent, or over 100 million, of all people who live in the United States can trace their roots to an ancestor who came through Ellis Island. And the United States still welcomes people from other countries. Every year about 130,000 professionals receive visas that give them the right to work in the United States.

AFTER READING

Circle all the words or phrases that answer each question.
Use the information given in the reading.
More than one answer may be correct.

1. From what parts of the world did many immigrants come to the United States in the early twentieth century?

   South America
   Southeast Asia
   southern Europe
   eastern Europe

2. Why was the trip across the ocean hard for immigrants?
   The compartments were crowded.
   They got seasick.
   They had no place to take showers.

3. What happened at Ellis Island?
   Immigrants got medical exams.
   U.S. officials asked immigrants questions.
   Families got information about the United States.
   People who were sick had to go back home.

4. What happened to many immigrants to the United States?
   They worked at low-paying jobs.
   They lived in country areas and worked on farms.
   They made a lot of money quickly and went back home.
   They lived in cities.

DISCUSSION

1. For what reasons do people move from one country to another?
2. Why do people call the United States a nation of many nations?
3. What problems do immigrants to new countries face?
4. Would you like to move to or live in a different country? Why or why not?

11 — WRITING

Write about yourself, your family, and your interests to someone in a different country.

> Dear Joe,
>
> I come from a big family. My father was the youngest of twelve children, and I have a brother and two sisters. I never knew my grandparents. They died before I was born. . . .

12 — PROJECT

> - Interview people who moved from one country to another and write about the stories.
> - Present your findings to the class.

2 CAREERS

LOOK AND LISTEN 🎧

Unusual Jobs

Personal Trainer

"I'm good at teaching people how to dance."

Yvonne Castillo works as a personal trainer in a fitness center in New York. She helps people with exercise plans. When she started teaching there two years ago, Yvonne found out that most of her students didn't enjoy working out on exercise equipment. It was very boring! So Yvonne, who used to be a professional dancer, had an idea. She combined music and dance steps. People are able to use the dance steps on walking equipment in the gym. Yvonne has been giving these kinds of lessons for over a year. One student says: "I've lost ten pounds, and I've been learning all kinds of different dance steps." Many people have hired her to give private lessons in their homes. Yvonne is thinking of opening her own center soon.

Tea Taster and Blender

"I'm good at testing teas."

Rachid Gandra is a tea taster and blender for an important company in London. He's been working in the tea business since he was a teenager. Rachid's job is to produce the various tea blends. The job requires great skill and a lot of experience. Rachid selects teas from as many as twenty different tea gardens and tastes them for quality, flavor, and color. Then he pours exactly 10 ounces of boiled water over 0.1765 ounces (5 grams) of tea, which is in a ceramic teapot. The liquid rests for precisely six minutes before he drinks it. Rachid tastes the tea and spits it out. Then he does a further test for the British market—he adds a little milk to the cup of tea.

Pearl Farmer and Merchant

"I'm good at selling. And I know how to produce good pearls."

Jean Duvalier has his own pearl farm on the island of Tahiti, in the South Pacific. Jean has been cultivating pearls for many years, and merchants come from all over the world to purchase his "black beauties" (as he calls them). To produce pearls, Jean and his workers place a small piece of shell in the oyster. The oyster covers the piece of shell with a pearly substance known as "nacre." This is the source of a pearl. The quality of a pearl depends on the environment in which the oyster lives: the temperature and quality of the water and food supply. Pearls that are smooth and have no spots or cracks sell for higher prices. Jean says that pearls are a gift of nature, and he finds his job fascinating.

Some not very common jobs	Requirements/skills
Gourmet writer	
Writes about and gives ratings to different restaurants and the foods they offer	Must have a good sense of taste, know a lot about food, enjoy eating, be a good writer, and like to travel
Private detective	
Investigates crimes for a fee and tries to get information for clients	Has to be discreet, be patient, pay attention to details, and be good at solving problems
Stockbroker	
Works in the stock market buying and selling shares	Must be able to make quick decisions, deal with stress, and be lucky
Test driver	
Test-drives new models and checks that cars are safe and free of problems before they go on the market	Needs to be an excellent driver, be critical, be very alert at every moment, and love cars
Your idea:	

1 — COMPREHENSION

Answer the questions. Write *true* or *false*.
1. ____ Yvonne works as a professional dancer.
2. ____ Yvonne has been giving exercise lessons for two years.
3. ____ Rachid grows plants for tea.
4. ____ Rachid has just started to work as a tea taster.
5. ____ Jean raises oysters for pearls.
6. ____ Jean sells all his pearls at the same price.

2 — PAIR WORK 🎧

A Ask and answer about the people.

- How long has *Yvonne* been working *as a personal trainer*?
- She's been working *as a personal trainer for two years*.

B Ask and answer about the jobs on these pages.

- What does a *gourmet writer* do?
- He/She *writes about food*.

- What skills do you need to be *a detective*?
- You must *pay attention to details*.

C Ask and answer about yourself.

- How long have you been *studying English*?
- I've been *studying English since I was six years old*.

- What jobs are you interested in?
- I'm interested in *working in the entertainment business*.
  I'm good at *singing and dancing*.

11

3 GRAMMAR

Present perfect progressive tense

The present perfect progressive describes an action that began in the past and that continues to the present.

Affirmative (+)

I've	(I + have)	
You've	(You + have)	
He's	(He + has)	been working for the company since 1995/for a long time.
She's	(She + has)	
We've	(We + have)	
They've	(They + have)	

Question (?)

Have	you	
Has	he/she	been waiting long?
Have	they	

Short answer (+)

	I	have.
Yes,	he/she	has.
	they	have.

Short answer (-)

	I	haven't.
No,	he/she	hasn't.
	they	haven't.

With some common verbs, either the present perfect or the present perfect progressive is commonly used: *drive, live, study, teach, work,* etc.

I've worked/I've been working for the ABC company for two years.

Adjective + preposition + gerund

I'm **good at using** computers.
I'm **interested in working** outdoors.
I'm not very **good at speaking** in public.
I'm not **interested in working** in the computer industry.

A Write answers to the following questions about your English study. Then ask a partner the questions.

1. How long have you been studying English?
2. How many teachers have you had?
3. How many books have you used?
4. How long have your been using *Super Goal*?

B Work with a partner. Make sentences. Follow the model.

Example:
Jack/photography studio/one year—taking pictures—photographer
Jack's been working at a photography studio for a year.
He's good at taking pictures, and he's interested in becoming a photographer.

1. Sally/cooking school/six months—bake things—chef
2. Nancy and Paul/film studio/a year—use camera—cinematographers
3. Lena/nursing home/two years—help people—nurse
4. Joe/newspaper/some time—interview people—reporter

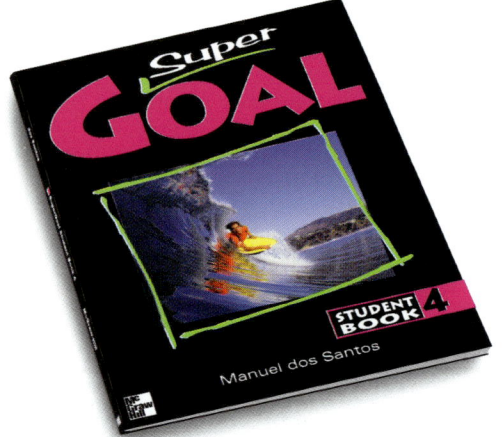

C Find out about your classmates' experiences, and ask how long they've been doing them.

Examples:
A: Can you ice-skate?
B: Yes, I can.
A: How long have you been doing it?
B: I've been ice-skating since I was five.

A: Do you work?
B: Yes, I do.
A: How long have you been working?
B: For about six months.

Activity	Name	Length of time
play a sport		
play a musical instrument		
study languages		
live in present house		
drive a car/ride a bike		
work part-time		
Your idea:		

D Work with a partner. Ask and answer questions about the picture: The road is blocked and workers are trying to fix it. People have been waiting for the road repairs. What have the people been doing during that time?

A: What has the engineer been doing?
B: He's been talking to the workers.

13

4 — GRAMMAR TALK

Prepare a job profile. Write down your qualifications, skills, and personality features.
In a group, discuss possible jobs for each student.

WORD BANK

Personality features
creative, efficient, friendly, hardworking, intelligent, organized, reliable, sociable, etc.

Good at or interested in
helping people
working alone
creating things
making a lot of money
working outdoors
working with people, etc.

Qualifications
degree in journalism

Personality
self-assured

Special skills
good at speaking in public

Possible job
TV announcer

Example:
A TV announcer **needs to be** self-assured and **has to be** comfortable in front of the cameras, and **should be** interested in following world events.

5 — LISTENING

A Listen to the job interview and complete the information.

CANDIDATE
Name: Michael Thomas
Education: _____
Skills: _____
Experience: _____

JOB APPLIED FOR
Working hours: _____
Salary: _____
Job description: _____

B DISCUSSION

Listen to the interview again. Do you think Michael will get the job? Why or why not?

6 — PRONUNCIATION

Listen and practice. Notice the differences in the sounds.

/m/	/n/	/ŋ/
model	bee**n**	worki**ng**
market	**n**urse	studyi**ng**

She's bee**n** worki**ng** as **m**odel.
He's bee**n** studyi**ng** to beco**m**e a **n**urse for a year.

7 — CHAT TIME

1. What do you plan do to after you finish school?
2. Do you have a job? How long have you been working in your present job?
3. What career would you like to follow? Why?
4. Have you ever had a job interview? Talk about it.
5. Have you ever had an internship? Talk about it.
6. Talk about the jobs you've had and the courses you've taken.
   Say how long you've been doing the jobs or taking the courses.

8 — CONVERSATION

CAREER CHANGES

Karen: I'm thinking of finding another job.

Ann: Oh! How long have you been working for the newspaper?

Karen: I've been working at the *Express* for almost five years. It's time to move on. Writing a gossip column about the rich and famous all the time gets boring.

Ann: I guess so, but you get to go to all those fantastic receptions and meet some fascinating people.

Karen: Well, I'd like to write something a bit more creative. I might work in advertising. I think it's a real challenge to create slogans for new products, and I might be good at coming up with them.

Ann: I've been looking for a new job. I want to move to a company where I can grow. I have special skills: I can speak foreign languages; I'm good at communicating with people; I'm good at solving problems; I'm organized, reliable, hardworking . . . What do you think?

YOUR ENDING

What advice does Karen give Ann?

① Why don't you send your résumé to different places?
② You should go to an employment agency.
③ Why don't we start our own company?
④ Your idea: _____

ABOUT THE CONVERSATION

1. What are Karen's and Ann's jobs?
2. Why does Karen want to change jobs? What does she want to do?
3. Why does Ann want to change jobs? What does she want to do?

9 — YOUR TURN

A Work with a partner. Act out the conversation between Karen and Ann. Then change the jobs to ones that interest you.

B Do the following role play: Interview either Karen or Ann a year later. Ask what she's been doing and what changes have occurred in her career. Present your interview to the class.

10 READING

BEFORE READING
1. What do you know about internships?
2. How do people find jobs? Do you know anyone who found a job on the Internet?

What's the Job for Me?

Media Intern: TV and Radio Media International

Do you want to be part of the fast-paced world of television—and meet famous people at the same time? Here's your chance. Our interns research information about hot topics in sources such as the Internet. They need to find information quickly and be able to summarize it in clear language. Our hosts use the information on their programs. Our interns also greet our guests when they arrive in our studios. You need to be fluent in English and be good at using computers. And you must be friendly and outgoing. This is a paid internship for the summer.
E-mail us at internship@radiomedia.com.

Archaeological Interns: Students Learning Overseas

Here's an opportunity to look at history firsthand and to work with noted archaeologists on an exciting dig. We've been uncovering ruins at the famous ancient city of Pompeii for several years. Interns' job is to dig slowly and carefully. They also work to uncover buildings that have been buried for centuries. It is very hard and painstaking work. The reward is a chance to discover something that the volcano Vesuvius buried with its lava two thousand years ago. This is an unpaid three-month internship, but lodging and meals are provided near the site. Join our team. Send us a résumé and cover letter.

Environmental Engineering: Mato Grosso, Brazil

Great opportunity for civil engineering graduate student in the area of environment. This project involves the construction of a road and a large number of bridges across the Parana River waterway. The interns work alongside experienced civil engineers and receive training in the different work sectors. You need to be able to read blueprints, have some knowledge of Portuguese or Spanish, and be able to cope with temperatures which average 104° Fahrenheit (40° Celsius) in the summer. Food and accommodations will be provided.
Send applications to: EE@Parana.com

To: internship@radiomedia.com
From: Mjohnson@homesite.com

Dear Sir or Madam:

I would like to apply for the internship position that you advertised on the Internet.

I believe that I have the right qualifications for the job. I've been working on my school newspaper for two years. During this time, I've been doing research for articles. I have experience in checking information from printed sources and from interviews. I've used word-processing programs for my work on the newspaper.

I'm interested in this internship because I'm thinking about pursuing a career in media. Right now I'm one of the hosts of a program for teens on our local radio station. This internship can offer me a great opportunity to meet people and make contacts.

I can send you references, and I am enclosing a copy of my résumé and of articles that I've written.

Very truly yours,
Michaela Johnson

Résumé

Name: Michaela Johnson
Address: 154 Tree Lane, Teaneck, New Jersey 07666
Phone Number: (201) 445-9899

EDUCATION: High school senior at City High School

EXPERIENCE:
- Reporter for high school newspaper "School Days"
  Have written articles on community issues and on student concerns
  Have done interviews and research to get background information
- Host of teen show on WXPX radio
  Interview people about teen-related issues on the air
  Decide on topics and help organize the show

HONORS/AWARDS:
- Edited school newspaper that won an award as one of the best in the state
- Wrote local newspaper article about jobs for teens

SKILLS:
- Know how to use a computer, including word-processing programs

AFTER READING
Answer *true* or *false*.
1. _____ The media intern needs to speak several languages.
2. _____ Archaeological interns get a good salary.
3. _____ The candidate must be good at reading blueprints to get the engineering job.
4. _____ Michaela has experience with word-processing programs.
5. _____ One of Michaela's articles has appeared in newspapers all over the country.

DISCUSSION
In your opinion, what makes a person qualified for a job?

11 — WRITING
Choose one of the ads for internships on page 16 and write a letter of application for it.
Or find an ad for an internship or a job on the Internet or in a newspaper and write a letter of application for it.

> Dear Sir or Madam:
>
> I'm writing about the position advertised in . . .

12 — PROJECT

- In a group, discuss your education, experience, and skills.
- Write your résumé, or the résumé you would like to have.
- Present your résumé to the group or to the class.

3 WHAT WILL BE WILL BE

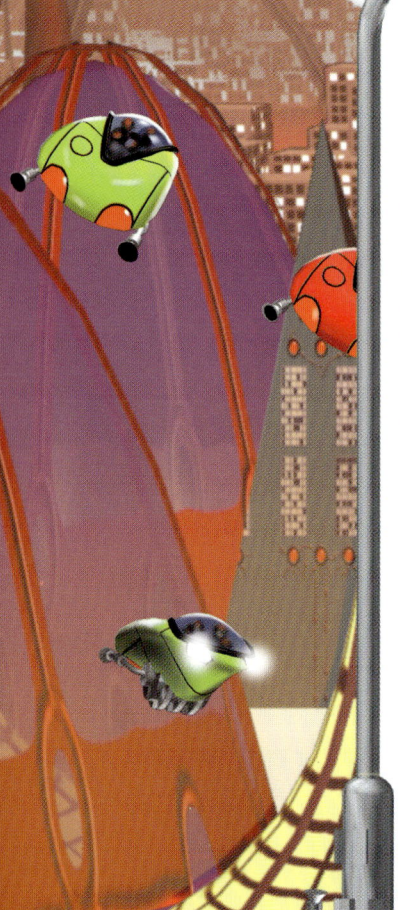

LOOK AND LISTEN

A Vision of the Future

The French writer Jules Verne wrote several books in the late 1800s. In them, he wrote about the future. He asked, "What will life be like at the end of the twentieth century—one hundred years from now?" In one of his adventure novels, his characters traveled to the moon in a rocket. In another novel, his characters dove in the depths of the ocean in a submarine in the shape of a whale. In a novel titled *Paris in the Twentieth Century,* Verne described a city with skyscrapers of glass and steel, high-speed trains, gas-powered automobiles, and a global communications network. Space rockets, submarines, and the other objects didn't exist in Verne's time, but many of the inventions in his novels became reality by the end of the 1900s. That's why people call Verne a visionary.

Here are ideas people have about life in the twenty-first century. In your opinion, which things do you think will probably come true?

- There will be fewer diseases, and life expectancy will be ninety to one hundred years.
- By the year 2100, people will be working four hours a day and will retire at the age of fifty.
- People will have more free time and will be traveling to other planets on vacation.
- People won't have any privacy, because computers will monitor their lives.
- The world will be at peace, and everyone will be speaking Chinese.
- Robots will do all the housework in the home, and they will perform most of the work in factories and offices.
- All the traffic will be in the air.
- Your idea: _____

1 COMPREHENSION

Write **V** for a prediction from Jules Verne. Write **B** for a prediction for the twenty-first century made on these pages.

1. ____ People won't drive cars on the ground.
2. ____ People will travel deep under the ocean in submarines.
3. ____ People will work only twenty hours a week.
4. ____ People will live until they're one hundred.
5. ____ People will travel to other planets such as Mars.
6. ____ People will live in skyscrapers.

Please fasten your seatbelts. We'll be departing for Mars shortly.

Will you fill her up with H_2O?

Drink **VITANOL**
You'll look just as young at 100 as when you were 50.

We're having friends for dinner. We're going to eat around nine. Will you please make your special recipe, code #3465.

2 — PAIR WORK

A Ask and answer about life in the year 2100. Use information in the presentation. Give your own ideas.

- What will people's lives be like in the year 2100?
- People will live longer. The life expectancy will be ninety to one hundred years.

- What changes will there be in the world in the year 2100?
- I think there won't be any more cars. People will travel in the air, not on the ground.

B Express your opinions about the future. It's the year 2025.

- What will your life be like in the year 2025?
- I'll be working as computer programmer, and I'll be traveling a lot around the world.

- Will life be better or worse in the year 2025?
- The way I see it, life will be easier, but people's feelings and hopes will be the same.

19

3 GRAMMAR

Future with: *will* or *be going to*

Use *will* or *be going to* to make predictions about the future.

Affirmative (+)
Computers **will perform** many functions.
People **are going to have** more free time.

Negative (-)
Computers **won't have** feelings.
Machines **aren't going to control** us.

Question (?)
Will people **eat** artificial food?
Are they **going to travel** to other planets?

Opinions
I guess so.   I hope not.
I think so.   I don't think so.

Note: The use of **shall** with *I* or *we* to express future time is formal and not very usual.
I **shall/will** see you tomorrow.
Will is also used in requests: **Will** you make dinner?

Will vs. *be going to*

Use *be going to* (not *will*) to express a preconceived plan.

What are your vacation plans?   I'**m going to** spend a month in . . .

Future progressive tense

Use the future progressive for continuous actions in the future.

Affirmative (+)
(At) this time tomorrow I'**ll be swimming in the ocean**.   or   I'm going to be swimming
A week from today I'**ll be relaxing** on the beach.   I'm going to be relaxing
By the year 3000, people **will be living** to the age of 120.   . . . are going to be living

Questions (?)
Will you be working on the weekend?
Are they going to be taking the test too?

Short answer (+)
Yes, I will.
Yes, they are.

Short answer (-)
No, I won't.
No, they aren't.

The present after *when*

Use the present after the *when* clause in a sentence.

When people **are not** home, robots will do all the housework.

A Complete each sentence with the correct verb form. More than one answer is possible.

1. In a hundred years, people _____ (live) on other planets.
2. Students _____ (study) with computers instead of books.
3. Cars _____ (not run) on gasoline.
4. Robots _____ (not control) peoples' lives.
5. Young people _____ (listen) to rock and roll only.
6. When your children _____ (be) adults, they _____ (drive) in the air.
7. When people _____ (reach) the age of fifty, they _____ (be) "young."

B Work in groups. Answer this question:
Which of the following do you think people will still be using in fifty years?
Explain why or why not.

telephone

fax machine

personal computer

ballpoint pen

VCR

magazines

C Work with a partner. Ask and answer.
Which of the following world problems do you think will be solved in this century?

Researchers will find a cure for cancer.
They'll find a vaccine for AIDS.
People will preserve nature.
Global warming will melt the ice at the poles.
There won't be any more pollution.
There won't be any more hunger.
There won't be any more war.
World population won't increase.

A: Do you think there will be enough food for everyone?
B: I believe there will be.
A: Do you believe there will be peace on Earth?
B: I don't. Nations are too selfish.

4 — GRAMMAR TALK

In which areas do you think there will be the most progress/advancements in this century? Write down your predictions and compare with a partner.

A: I believe medicine will make the most advances in this century. Doctors will transplant more and more artificial organs.

B: I disagree. I think telecommunications will have the greatest advances. People will be using telepathy to communicate. They will be able to communicate their thoughts directly to another person.

Areas: education, health, transportation, communications, work, leisure
Future changes: _____

5 — LISTENING

Listen to the principal's speech and complete the chart about the students' past and future.

Name	Past	Future
Jimmy		
Miriam		
Jeff		
Sarah		

6 — PRONUNCIATION

Listen and practice. Note the words that are not usually stressed.

a	in a century	**to**	five to eight
and	young and old	**was**	it was late
can	cars can fly	**of**	the car of the future

7 — CHAT TIME

1. Do you believe in predictions?
2. Do you believe people can tell the future?
3. Do you know of any predictions that came true?
4. Do you have any New Year's resolutions? Do you keep them?
5. What changes do you foresee for this century?
6. What do you think you'll be doing twenty years from now?

8 — CONVERSATION

Host: Will you tell us about the new intelligent home your company has built? It promises to be a model for the houses of the future.

Grace: Certainly. The idea is not to have a house full of gadgets. This is a complete household system. It will make people's lives easier.

Host: OK. So tell me how this house will make my life easier?

Grace: When you arrive at the front door, you won't need a key. The door will open with a touch of your finger: the system recognizes your fingerprint. You'll be able to call your refrigerator when you're in the supermarket and find out how much milk you still have and figure out how much you need to buy. Isn't that wonderful?

Host: Can I call the washing machine as well?

Grace: Sure. But you won't need to. The house comes with a robot. Greeves has been programmed to do the cleaning, the washing, and the ironing.

Host: What about household problems?

Grace: Well, if a pipe bursts, the house will call the plumber. And if there's a fire, the house will turn on the fire extinguishers automatically and call the fire department.

Host: And what's the price of this intelligent home?

Grace: A million dollars.

Host: A million dollars! It will be the twenty-second century before I'll be able to afford to buy one!

ABOUT THE CONVERSATION
1. What are some features of the intelligent house?
2. Why will someone who owns the house call the refrigerator?
3. What is the role of the robot?
4. What are some safety features of the house?

9 — YOUR TURN

A Role-play the conversation with a partner. Use the following prompts.

| key | refrigerator | robots | household problems | price |

Decide on one or two additional features for the house and add them to your role play.

B Do the following role play:
You are the owner of the intelligent house and a friend is visiting you.
Explain the features of the intelligent and why you like them.
Use your imagination and invent more details for the house.

10 READING

BEFORE READING

What do you know about the Beatles? Discuss with a partner.

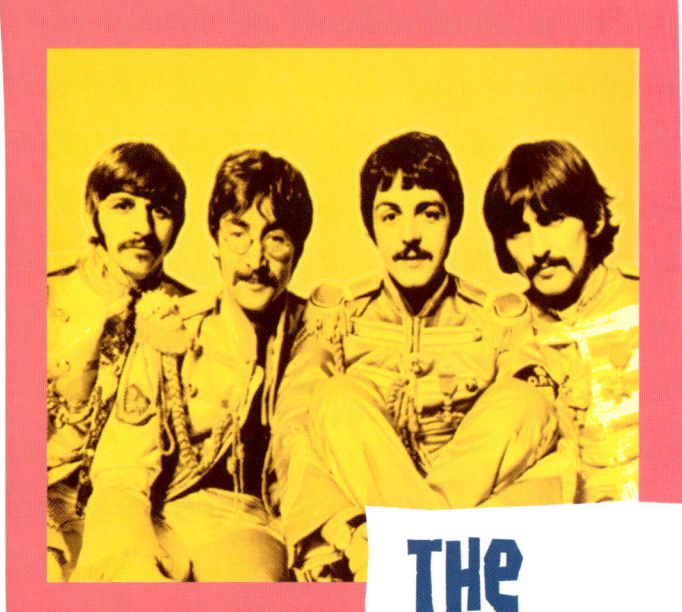

THE BEATLES

The four "lads" (boys) from Liverpool—John, Paul, George, and Ringo—revolutionized music in the sixties and influenced the behavior and thought of a whole generation. John Lennon and Paul McCartney wrote music that people have been playing and enjoying for over thirty years. *Rolling Stone* magazine and *MTV* both considered "Yesterday"—one of the Beatles' songs—one of the most beautiful pop songs of all times. But will people be playing their songs in two hundred years? Will the Beatles be remembered in the future as important composers of all time—along with classical composers like Mozart and Beethoven? Paul McCartney will probably wonder: "Will you still love me, will you still hear me, in 2204?"

READING ★

Songs and poetry in English often rhyme. This means that the sounds at the end of words are the same. Can you find the rhyming words in the Beatles' song?

When I'm Sixty-Four
JOHN LENNON and PAUL McCARTNEY

When I get older losing my hair
Many years from now.
Will you still be sending me a Valentine,
Birthday greetings, bottle of wine?
If I'd been out till quarter to three
Would you lock the door?
Will you still need me,
Will you still feed me,
When I'm sixty-four?
You'll be older too,
And if you say the word,
I could stay with you.
I could be handy mending a fuse
When your lights have gone.
You can knit a sweater, by the fireside,
Sunday mornings, go for a ride.
Doing the garden, digging the weeds,
Who could ask for more?
Will you still need me,
Will you still feed me,
When I'm sixty-four?
Every summer we can rent a cottage,
In the Isle of Wight, if it's not too dear.
We shall scrimp and save.
Grandchildren on your knee,
Vera, Chuck and Dave.
Send me a postcard, drop me a line
Stating point of view.
Indicate precisely what you mean to say,
Yours sincerely wasting away.
Give me your answer, fill in a form,
Mine for evermore.
Will you still need me,
Will you still feed me,
When I'm sixty-four?

BEATLES

AFTER READING

A Choose the right answer.

1. Who is the "I" in the song?
   a. a young person
   b. an old person

2. The "I" is talking to
   a. a girlfriend/boyfriend
   b. a new acquaintance

3. The "I" wants to
   a. end a relationship
   b. make the relationship permanent

4. One of the things "I" suggests they do in the future is
   a. work in the garden
   b. go shopping

B Match the words with their meaning.
1. ____ dear   a. useful with one's hands
2. ____ drop a line   b. small house
3. ____ dig the weeds   c. write a short letter
4. ____ cottage   d. expensive
5. ____ handy   e. remove wild plants
6. ____ scrimp and save   f. try to spend as little money as possible

DISCUSSION
1. What question is the person asking in the song? What's the problem?
2. What request does the person make at the end
3. What questions does he/she ask about the future?
4. What things does the "I" in the song ask the other person to do?

11 — WRITING

Write about what music will be like in the future or what things that are popular today will still be popular in the future.

I think that the Volkswagen Beetle will still be running in the future.

12 — PROJECT

- *Find a song that is popular or well-known today and that you think will be popular in fifty years. It can be a new song or an old song.*
- *Present your song to the class and say why you think it will be popular in the future.*

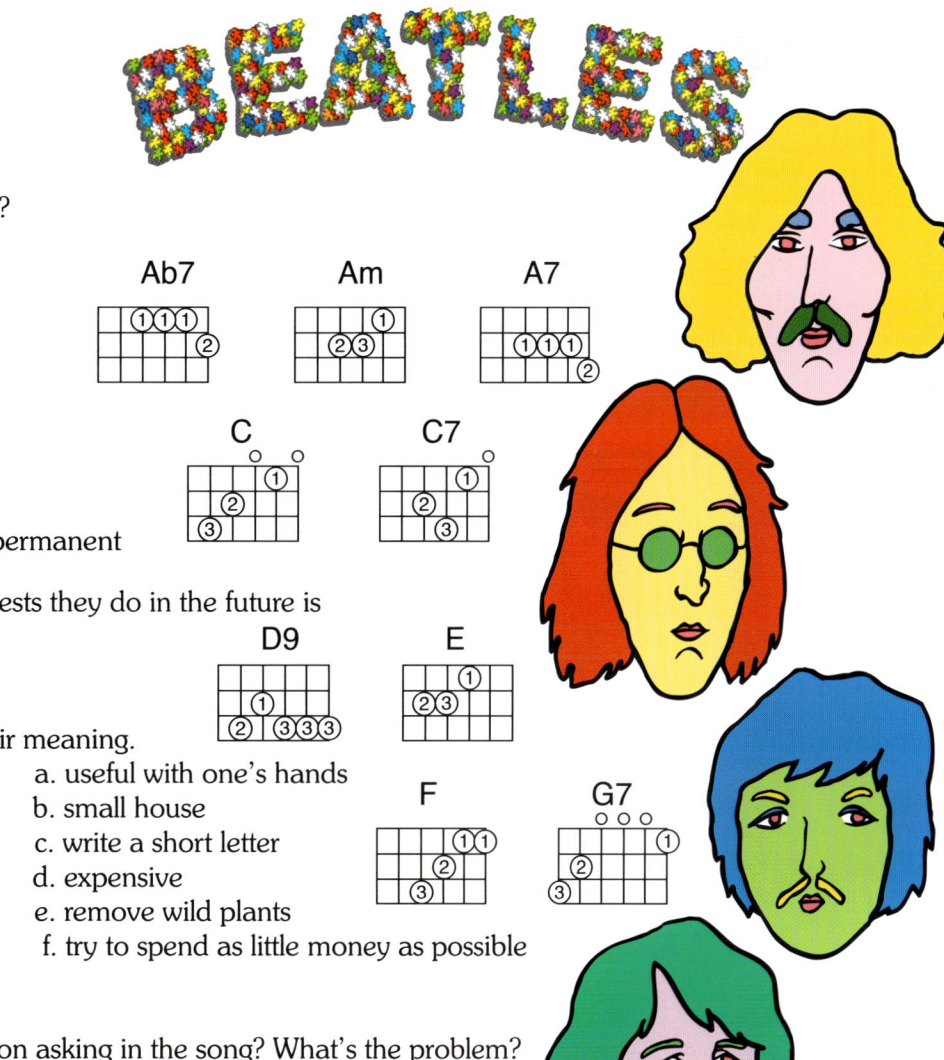

EXPANSION 1

1 — READING

BEFORE READING
1. What do you understand from the title?
2. What forms of body decoration do you know about?

DECORATING THE BODY

Do you notice people on the street with brightly colored red or blue hair or people on the beach with pictures or patterns painted on their bodies? You might think that these are the latest trends. Well, think again. People have used color decoration on their bodies for a long long time.

In fact, recently scientists have found the remains of a culture that dates back 80,000 to 100,000 years in a cave on the southern part of South Africa. In this cave, called Blombos Cave, they found some of the oldest tools of stone and bone. But more important, they found a lot of ochre—a red-colored iron ore. Scientists say that some pieces of the ochre look like crayons for drawing. Most scientists think that prehistoric people used the pieces of ochre to draw symbolic decorations on their bodies. Some scientists think that people painted their bodies to be attractive to members of the opposite sex. Scientists can also trace makeup back 10,000 years to ancient Egypt. The ancient Egyptians used to grind colored stones like green malachite into powders that they rubbed on their eyelids. Both men and women used this eye makeup to be more attractive. More than 1,000 years ago, the ancient Celts in Britain dyed their hair with bright colors—most often red, but sometimes bright blue.

Some of these ancient traditions continue into the twenty-first century. People in some cultures use them for special occasions. In the West African nation of Niger, a group of nomads have a kind of beauty contest that extends for one week every year. Males paint their faces with bright makeup and wear elaborate costumes. They draw bright lines down their noses and paint patterns of white dots on their cheeks. They are judged on looks and personality by women from neighboring groups. In other cultures, the use of body painting is a bit more serious, and it sometimes marks passages in an individual's life. In India and Pakistan, the use of henna—a plant that is able to dye any surface—is common for rituals before marriage. Brides' hands are painted with beautiful patterns in henna. The body painting marks the woman as special. In New Zealand, the indigenous people, the Maori, have long used facial tattoos to show which community they belonged to and their place in that community. Tattooing is adding permanent color to the skin by putting pigment under the skin or by cutting the skin to make scars. The traditional Maori facial tattoos had beautiful curving lines, and some Maoris who want to preserve their heritage still get tattoos today.

So, those latest fashions in bright body colors may not be so new after all. They are following traditions that actually date from the earliest humans.

AFTER READING

A Answer about the text.
1. What are the latest trends mentioned in the text?
2. How long have people been decorating their bodies?
3. What does the beauty contest in Niger consist of?
4. How long have Egyptians worn makeup?
5. How did the Egyptians produce makeup?
6. What did the Celts use to do?

B Complete the following sentences.
1. Many scientists believe that our ancestors used ochre _____.
2. Prehistoric people used to paint their bodies _____.
3. Body painting is used in India and Pakistan _____.
4. Some Maoris today still tattoo their bodies, because _____.

2 — TALK ABOUT IT

1. What different forms of body decoration do people use in your country?
2. Which are the most popular forms?
3. What do you think about tattoos, body piercing, and coloring your hair?

3 — ACTIVITIES

A How long have people been wearing the following items?

Example: People have been wearing/have worn footwear for 5,000 years.

Perforated animal teeth, which may have been worn as necklaces or bracelets, have been found on sites dating back over 40,000 years.

The famous Ice Age statuettes known as the Venus of Willendorf and of Brassempouy show clear evidence of stylized hair, and these may be 30,000 years old.

Corsets were used by women to constrict their waists and enhance their busts in Minoan times (1800 B.C.).

The necktie style began in 1660 when Louis XIV presented a group of Croatian soldiers with a red handkerchief to wear around the neck. The word *cravat* comes from *Croat*.

Ladies' fashionable hats were very popular among the nobility and upper-class society in the 1700s.

Men's top hats were adopted in the 1830s and were most often made of silk.

Athletic shoes came into existence around 1900, when Joseph William Foster designed a running shoe. Foster started a shoe company, which later became Reebok.

The miniskirt was created in the 60s by designer Mary Quant. The fashion has come and gone ever since.

B Which of the above items do you think people will wear/will still be wearing in the future/in 200 years?

Example: I think people will still wear ties in 200 years.
　　　　　　I don't think people will still be wearing ties in the future.

C Think about current fads.
  1. Make a list of current fads.
  2. Survey your classmates about which they like and which they don't like.

Fad	Name	Yes	No

4 — WRITING

Write the history of a clothing item or a brand name item.

29

4 ONLY THE BEST

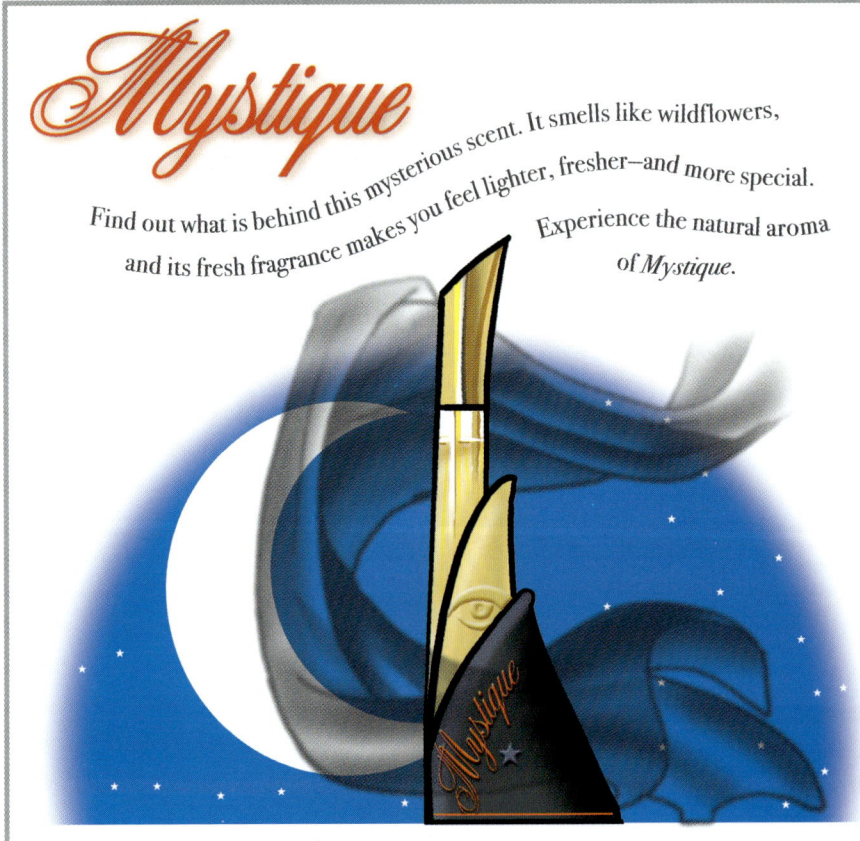

LOOK AND LISTEN

The Smaller, the Better — Bee

It looks fantastic and it's impossible to live without.

The *Bee car* is one of the world's smallest and most compact cars. It was designed by a group of engineers in Italy and France. It was put through all kinds of tests, and it has been proven to be one of the safest and strongest small cars ever. The Bee was built with as many safety features as most luxury cars, and special attention was paid to materials and the effect the car has on environment. It comes with a .650-liter engine, seats two people comfortably, and has a good-sized trunk. The Bee is fun to drive. It is inexpensive to buy and economical to run. It is also versatile—and fashionable: accessories such as bumpers, doors, and wheels of different colors can be blended to match each person's taste and style. But the greatest advantage of the Bee is that it can be parked in a very small space.

Mystique

Find out what is behind this mysterious scent. It smells like wildflowers, and its fresh fragrance makes you feel lighter, fresher—and more special. Experience the natural aroma of *Mystique*.

About Perfume

Of all the senses, none is so mysterious as that of smell. Perfumes are made from parts of flowers and many other pleasant-smelling substances, such as herbs, spices, woods, fruits, and oils. The Egyptians were the first to introduce perfume into their culture, and some special perfumes were considered more precious than gold. Perfume was used by the rulers of ancient Egypt (when the tomb of Tutankhamen was opened there was an odor of perfume). In Persia, perfume was considered a sign of high rank or class. The Greeks said that it was invented by the gods. In Rome, scent was used extravagantly in the famous baths and during banquets. Muhammad promised his followers the Garden of Paradise, a place where the most exotic perfumes are found. It was used in ancient India, China, and Japan. In fact, perfume has been used by all the ancient and modern cultures. But the first perfume to have a designer's name was Chanel No. 5, in its famous Art Deco bottle. Coco Chanel's perfume was launched in 1923.

What do these two bikes have in common?

They were made by the world's largest and most trusted bicycle company.

The Trenton Racing Bike

Bicycles were invented in France in the 1790s. They were made of wood, had a front wheel that didn't move, and had no pedals. In 1817, a steerable front wheel was developed by Baron Karl von Drais in Germany, and in 1839, the first pedals were introduced by Kirkpatrick MacMillan, a blacksmith from Scotland. The first bikes had large front wheels because it was believed that the bigger the front wheel, the faster the bike.

The Trenton Company was started by Sir Christopher Trenton in 1895 in London, England, and it has been making bikes ever since. Our first racing bike was made in 1898, and it reached a speed of 25 miles (40 kilometers) per hour. Recently one of our bikes reached 75 miles (120 kilometers) an hour in the *Tour de France*.

Today Trenton bikes are made of the lightest and most resistant materials, and they are available in a great variety of models and sizes.

1 — COMPREHENSION

Answer *true* or *false*.

____ 1. The Bee car is smaller than other cars.
____ 2. The Bee car was designed in Asia.
____ 3. The Bee car can be parked in a small place.
____ 4. Perfume has been used for thousands of years.
____ 5. Perfumes have long been named for their designers.
____ 6. Perfumes were very expensive and were considered special.
____ 7. Bicycles were invented one hundred years ago.
____ 8. Old bikes were made with large front wheels to go faster.
____ 9. Racing bikes are no longer made by the Trenton Company.

2 — PAIR WORK

A Ask and answer about the products.

- What is *the Trenton bike* made of?
- *The ad says that it's made of the lightest materials.*

- When *were bikes* invented/first used?
- *They were invented in the eighteenth century.*

B Make comparisons about the products.

- How are modern bikes different from old bikes?
- *They're lighter than old bikes.*

C Discuss the special features of products.

- What's special about *the Bee*?
- *The Bee is the smallest car produced.*

D Choose a product that you like.
Why is it special?
Write down two reasons.
Share them with a partner.

31

3 GRAMMAR

The passive

Use the passive to emphasize what was done instead of who did it.
The passive is formed by combining a form of the verb **to be** with the past participle.

Simple present:	This car **is made** in Japan.
Simple past:	This perfume **was developed** in France.
Present perfect:	Our bikes **have been used** by cyclists all over the world.
Future:	A cure for AIDS **will be found** by researchers.

Note: Sometimes the doer of the action is put after the preposition **by**.

Comparatives and superlatives

Adjective	**Comparative form**	**Superlative form**
The Bee car is **safe**.	It's **safer** than other cars.	It's the **safest** car on the road.
The Bee car is **compact**.	It's **more compact** than others.	It's the **most compact** car there is.

Verbs *look, smell, sound, taste* with *like* + noun

Use **like** + noun with the verbs **look, smell, sound, taste** to describe and compare things.

The Bee car **looks like** a bee.   That **sounds like** a good idea.
This perfume **smells like** roses.   Frog legs **taste like** chicken.

A Change the sentences from active to passive.

Example:

A company in Japan makes the car.   *The car is made by . . .*
A company in Japan made the car.   *The car was made by . . .*
A company in Japan has made the car for two years.   *The car has been made by . . .*
A company in Japan will make the car.   *The car will be made by . . .*

1. Karl Benz made the first car in 1886.
2. Companies all over the world produce cars nowadays.
3. In the future, people will drive smaller and smaller cars.
4. Cartier makes perfume, watches, and jewelry.
5. Francois Coty started the perfume industry in the late 1800s.
6. The French have produced famous perfumes for many years.
7. People of all ages will spend a lot of money on perfume.
8. Factories make bikes from steel, plastic, and other materials.
9. In the past, many people used bikes to go to work.

B Complete the paragraphs. Use the correct form of the passive.

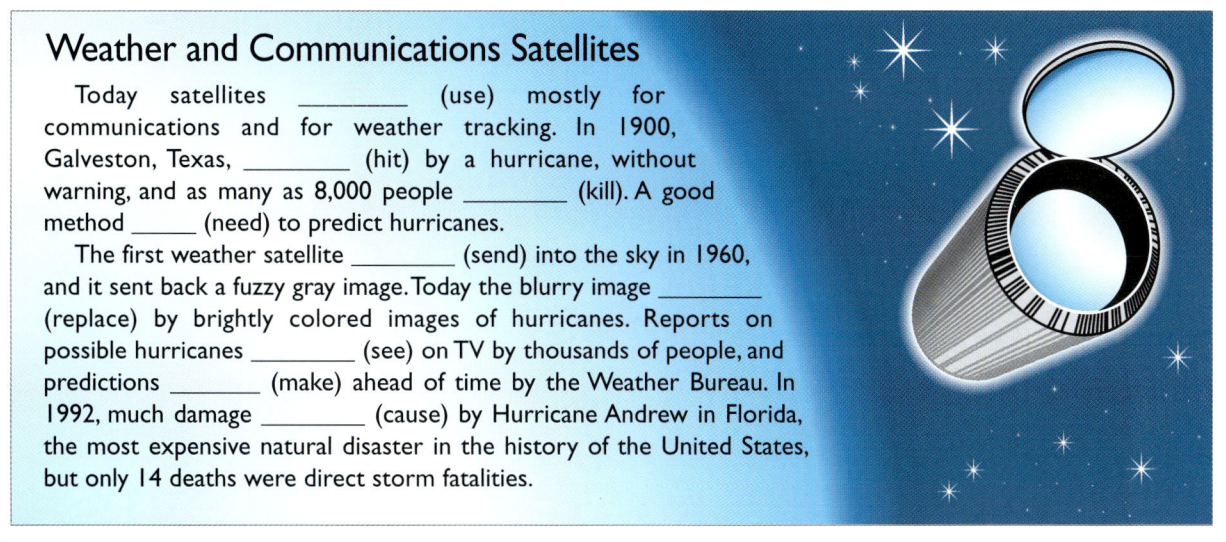

Weather and Communications Satellites

Today satellites _____ (use) mostly for communications and for weather tracking. In 1900, Galveston, Texas, _____ (hit) by a hurricane, without warning, and as many as 8,000 people _____ (kill). A good method _____ (need) to predict hurricanes.

The first weather satellite _____ (send) into the sky in 1960, and it sent back a fuzzy gray image. Today the blurry image _____ (replace) by brightly colored images of hurricanes. Reports on possible hurricanes _____ (see) on TV by thousands of people, and predictions _____ (make) ahead of time by the Weather Bureau. In 1992, much damage _____ (cause) by Hurricane Andrew in Florida, the most expensive natural disaster in the history of the United States, but only 14 deaths were direct storm fatalities.

C Complete the ads with the comparative or superlative forms of the adjectives.

Bliss
The _____ (refreshing) fragrance for night and day. Members of the opposite sex will be attracted to anyone with the scent.

Sparkle Toothpaste
Sparkle makes your teeth _____ (clean) and _____ (bright) than ever.

Homemade Foods
What's good for the pet is good for the owner.
Your dog and cat will look _____ (healthy) when they eat this food.

XX
Double X, the _____ (reliable) of all pocket PCs.
The new pocket PC was designed for mobility and efficiency.

D Now complete the sentences about the ads. Share your answers with a partner.
1. If you use Bliss, _____.
2. If you buy Homemade pet food, _____.
3. If you use Sparkle, _____.
4. If you want mobility and efficiency in a pocket PC, _____.

E In your opinion, which is the best ad? Compare with a partner.

4 GRAMMAR TALK

A How good is your general knowledge? Choose the correct answer. How many points did you get?

1. ____ Ice cream was invented
2. ____ The *Mona Lisa* was painted
3. ____ *Hamlet* was written
4. ____ Coca-Cola was invented
5. ____ The law of gravity was discovered
6. ____ The first Volkswagen was designed
7. ____ The telephone was invented
8. ____ The first 200 Bibles were printed
9. ____ The ballpoint pen was made famous
10. ____ The first razor blade was produced

a. by John Pembleton in 1886 in Atlanta.
b. by King Camp Gillette in 1903.
c. by Gutenberg in 1455 in Germany.
d. by the Chinese 4,000 years ago.
e. by Leonardo da Vinci.
f. by the Hungarian Biro.
g. by William Shakespeare.
h. by Ferdinand Porsche in the early 1930s.
i. by Isaac Newton.
j. by Alexander Graham Bell in 1876.

B Share any information you have on the topics in small groups.

Points:
9 – 10 Excellent
6 – 8 Good
5 – 7 Not bad
0 – 4 Weak

5 LISTENING

Listen to the ads and match.

1. ____ *Sunray* is
2. ____ *Sparkle* is
3. ____ *NoAche* is
4. ____ *Spotless* is

a. an effective pain killer.
b. a lotion used to protect your skin.
c. a washing soap which removes all the dirt and smell.
d. a soft drink which provides a lot of energy.

6 PRONUNCIATION

Listen and practice. Note the overuse of stress on certain words for emphasis and exaggeration.

fabulous	The Bee is a **fab**ulous car.
fan**tas**tic	This perfume has a fan**tas**tic smell.
wonderful	The car is a **won**derful color.

7 CHAT TIME

Listen to the ads and match.

1. Are you influenced by advertising? Think of a product that you bought because of an ad. What factors do you think influenced your decision?
2. What is false advertising? Can you give any examples of it?
3. What kinds of items shouldn't be advertised? Why not?
4. Do you think advertising standards should be stricter?
5. To what extent do you think ads influence children and teens, and people in general?
6. Talk about the best and the worst ad you've ever seen.

8 — CONVERSATION

Alex: What are you laughing about?
Vicki: I just saw the silliest ad on TV for jam and soups. It said: "All our products are homemade with the freshest vegetables and fruits." Then a scene in the factory showed that products were prepared and packed by the most sophisticated machinery.
Alex: And I bet the word "natural" was put on the jars and cans of the products. I think the stupidest ads are those that imply that "you're one of a kind." If you buy the product, you'll be a very special person. No, you'll be just like every other one of the twenty million people who bought it.
Vicki: That's really silly! But to me, the dumbest of them all is when advertisers put a celebrity on TV to talk about a particular brand of soap or about a particular car. I bet that the celebrities never used the product before they got the job of appearing in the commercial.
Alex: Yeah, but most of these commercials work, and people remember the product.
Vicki: I agree. Here we are talking about ads we've seen, aren't we?

ABOUT THE CONVERSATION
1. What did the ad say about homemade products?
2. What was silly about the ad?
3. What does Alex think about "you're one of a kind" ads?
4. Which ads does Vicki think are the stupidest?

9 — YOUR TURN

A   Act out the conversation with a partner. Use the following prompts.

what/laugh	I think the stupidest ads/"you're one of a kind"
silliest ad/jams and soups	To me, the dumbest ads of all/celebrities

B   Work with a partner. Prepare two role plays. In one, talk about ads that you think are silly. In the other, talk about ads that you think are interesting.

10 READING

BEFORE READING

What do you know about hamburgers? Discuss in a group.

> **READING**
> To understand a reading, look at each paragraph carefully. Ask, "What is it about? What more does it tell me about the topic?"

FROM HAMBURG TO HAMBURGERS

People think that hamburgers were invented in the United States, but that is not totally true. These round flat cakes, or patties, made of ground beef actually came from Germany in the middle of the nineteenth century. They were brought to the United States by German immigrants who came from the city of Hamburg. That is why their name was "hamburger steak."

But what happened next isn't clear. The most popular story is that the hamburger was first put between two pieces of bread at the 1904 World's Fair in St. Louis. However, people in other places claim that they invented the hamburger. Perhaps we'll never have a clear answer. But there's no question that the hamburger was a hit. Why? Perhaps because at that time, industry was growing, and a kind of fast, practical, and cheap food was needed for workers. Or perhaps it was just because hamburgers tasted good.

The hamburger became even more popular in the 1920s when the first chain of fast food restaurants was started. This chain was called "White Castle." It served tiny hamburgers that were sold for the low price of 5 cents. A trend of the 1930s was the drive-in restaurant. Customers were served in their cars by waiters in uniform. And one of the most popular menu items was the hamburger.

By now, the hamburger was ready to conquer the world. And this happened with McDonald's, which was actually a hot-dog stand at first. But the hot dog was replaced by the hamburger by the early 1950s. At McDonald's, people were served quickly inside the restaurant. The drive-in concept changed, too. The waiters disappeared. People ordered from their cars, received their food quickly, and drove away. McDonald's and other fast food restaurants sprang up around the world throughout the rest of the twentieth century. Fast food restaurants that sell hamburgers can be found in Austria or Australia, Jamaica or Japan. McDonald's alone has sold twelve hamburgers for every person in the world.

The importance of the hamburger to U.S. culture remains significant. About 60 percent of all sandwiches that are eaten are hamburgers. According to some sources, 7 percent of current workers in the United States had their first job at McDonald's.

But the face of the hamburger is changing according to the times. Nowadays it is possible to buy a chicken burger, a turkey burger, a fish burger, or a veggie burger.

AFTER READING

A Match each topic with the correct paragraph.
Write the number of the paragraph.
1. _sixth_ Hamburgers have changed with the times.
2. _____ Hamburgers gained popularity in the United States, but they weren't invented there.
3. _____ The fast food restaurant concept was developed by McDonald's and spread throughout the world.
4. _____ The first fast food chain served hamburgers, and it was a success.
5. _____ Hamburgers and McDonald's remain an important part of U.S. culture.
6. _____ Why the hamburger gained popularity isn't clearly known.

B Find words in the text for each of the following definitions.
1. persons who go to another country to live there
2. place where goods and products are displayed
3. place where customers are served in their cars
4. clothes worn by members of a group
5. food that is inexpensive and is served quickly

C Summarize.
In your own words, tell the story of hamburgers. You can tell it to a partner or write it down.

LEARNING
Summarizing helps you remember what you read. It also helps you use the language you are learning.

11 — WRITING

Choose a product and write its history.

> The first sewing machine was made by the French tailor Barthélemy Thimonnier in 1830. It produced 200 stitches a minute against a human's mere twenty stitches. At the time, the tailors thought they were going to lose their jobs, so they destroyed Mr. Thimonnier's shop. Of course that didn't happen.

12 — PROJECT

> - Choose a product, and then write an advertisement for it.
> - Say if the ad is for the radio, TV, magazines or newspapers.
> - Think of an interesting slogan for the product.
> - You may want to use pictures to illustrate your ad.

5 DID YOU HURT YOURSELF?

LOOK AND LISTEN

I HATE FRYING. I KEEP BURNING MYSELF.

SO DO I. I BURNED MYSELF WHILE I WAS MAKING FRIES.

WHAT HAPPENED?

I SLIPPED AND HURT MYSELF. THE FLOOR WAS WET.

SO DID I. BUT I SLIPPED ON A RUG.

HOW DID YOU CUT YOURSELF?

THE CAN OPENER BROKE, SO I TRIED USING A KNIFE.

I'M TRYING TO FIX THIS LIGHT. I LIKE DOING THINGS MYSELF.

SO DO I. BUT JUST REMEMBER TO TURN OFF THE ELECTRICITY.

THAT WAS COOL! AND I DIDN'T HURT MYSELF.

NEITHER DID I. LET'S DO IT AGAIN!

COMMON ACCIDENTS

Facts on

Adolescent Injury
- The largest proportion of teen injuries is the result of motor vehicle crashes.
  1. Adolescents are far less likely to use seat belts than any other age group.
  2. More than 50 percent of adolescent fatalities in car accidents occur at night.
- Most injuries for teen workers occur in restaurants.
  1. Adolescents working in the restaurant industry are at six times greater risk of burning themselves than in any other job.
  2. The highest rate of such injuries occurs in hamburger restaurants (52.6 percent).

Child Injuries
In the home
There are many cases of accidents in the home. Young children might fall out of windows, play with matches, get an electric shock, or ingest poisonous substances. Young children often aren't aware of the dangers of everyday objects, so they don't use them with care. So keep objects out of children's reach, in case they try to play with them.

Playground-related injuries
Most injuries (60 percent) happen because children fall off swings, monkey bars, or slides.

Senior Citizen Injuries
Falls can happen at any time in any place to people of any age, but most falls by people who are sixty-five and older occur in the home.
- The most common results of falls are head injuries and fractures of the wrist and hip.
- Many falls are due to wet floors or slippery rugs. They often occur when people are walking on stairs or reaching for things on high shelves.

1 — COMPREHENSION

Look at the statements about accidents.
Check the true statements.

Teens
1. ____ Most teen injuries occur in drive-in restaurants.
2. ____ Most teen injuries occur in car accidents at night.

Children
1. ____ Children are safe at home. There are few dangers.
2. ____ Most injuries in playgrounds occur with playground equipment.

Senior Citizens
1. ____ Most falls for senior citizens occur in bad weather.
2. ____ The results of falls are often broken bones.

2 — PAIR WORK

A Ask and answer about people in the pictures.

- How did *the man in the emergency room* hurt *himself*?
- He slipped on a wet floor.

- And did *the children in the playground* hurt *themselves*?
- No, they didn't.

B Discuss any accidents you've had.
Share experiences with your partner.

- I once broke my arm.
- So did I. I fell off a swing.
- Hey, so did I.

- I've never been in a car accident.
- Neither have I.

C Use the information in the pictures and in Common Accidents to write sentences using *so* and *because*.

The woman cut herself because . . .

Most teen deaths are in car accidents, so teens . . .

3 — GRAMMAR

Reflexive pronouns

Use the reflexive pronoun when the subject and the object are the same person.

   myself
   yourself
   himself, herself, itself
   ourselves
   yourselves
   themselves

I like to look at **myself** in the mirror.

Note: We also use reflexive pronouns to say that we did something without anyone's help.
I fixed the car **myself/by myself**.

Because vs. *so*

The conjunction **because** introduces a reason—it tells why. The conjunction **so** introduces a consequence or result.

Most accidents happen **because** people don't pay attention.
He didn't turn off the electricity, **so** he got a shock.

If vs. *in case*

Use **if** to talk about cause and effect. Use **in case** to talk about precautions.

If you play with fire, you will/might get burned.
Insure your house **in case** there is a fire.

FYI *In case of* + noun: "Break glass in case of fire."

Verb + gerund or infinitive

Some verbs can be followed by either a gerund or an infinitive.
Sometimes there is a difference in meaning.

Verb	Meaning
He **tried to learn** English.	make an effort
He **tried learning** English with different books.	experiment in different ways but possibly not succeeding
She always **remembers to turn off** the light.	not forget a task
She **remembers turning off** the light before leaving.	recall what happened

So and *neither*

I hurt myself all the time.
So do I.

I burned myself on the stove.
So did I.

I've been in one car accident in my life.
So have I.

I very seldom cut myself.
Neither do I.

I didn't slip on the wet floor.
Neither did I.

I've never broken an arm or leg.
Neither have I.

A Complete the sentences. Use the correct reflexive pronoun.
1. My little sister cut _____ while she was peeling the potatoes.
2. The instructions on the machine say you can repair it _____ if it breaks down.
3. I burned _____ when I was cooking the roast.
   I told _____ to be more careful when I cooked.
4. My grandfather slipped on a rug and hurt _____.
5. The girls' house burned down. They hurt _____ when they were trying to escape.
6. We were spectators at the big fire, and we saw _____ on TV that night.
7. Tom and Jane, please look after _____ during the trip.
8. The dog burned _____, because it tried to eat the food while it was still hot.

B Join the sentences with *so* and *because*.

Example:
He burned his arm. He went to the emergency room.

He burned his arm, **so** he went to the emergency room.
He went to the emergency room **because** he burned his arm.

1. The floor was wet. Mary slipped and fell.
2. Julian wasn't wearing a seat belt. He hit his head on the windshield.
3. The baby put his finger in the socket. He got an electric shock.
4. There wasn't any water to put out the fire. We had to use sand.
5. Janna was riding too fast. She fell off her bike.
6. I got my hands all blue. I didn't read the "wet paint" sign.

C Choose the correct meaning.

1. I remember turning off the oven.
   a. I know I turned off the oven.
   b. I never forget to turn off the oven.

2. She no longer ate chocolate.
   a. She stopped buying chocolate on the way home.
   b. On the way home, she stopped to buy some chocolate.

3. My father finally gave up smoking.
   a. My father stopped smoking cigarettes.
   b. My father stopped to smoke a cigarette.

4. Mary tried fixing the lamp, but she didn't know how.
   a. She worked on fixing the lamp and she was able to fix it.
   b. She worked on fixing the lamp and she wasn't successful.

4 — GRAMMAR TALK

What do you think will happen in the following situations?
  Examples:
  If he doesn't wear a mask, he'll/he might hurt his eyes.
  He should wear a mask **in case** sparks get into his eyes and injure them.

5 — LISTENING

Dr. Sinclair is a child psychologist.

A Listen. Mark the items she refers to in her talk.

pills		sockets	
knives		benders	
soft drinks		bathroom	
matches		refrigerator	
cooker		pots and pans	
windows		superheroes	

B Listen again.
What does she say about the following topics?
1. Children's curiosity
2. Keeping things out of the reach of children
3. The kitchen
4. The balcony
5. Teaching children how to deal with danger

6 — PRONUNCIATION

Listen and practice. These are common consonant clusters at the end of words.

/lf/	/lt/	/nt/	/st/	/nd/
myse**lf**	resu**lt**	accide**nt**	wri**st**	a**nd**
she**lf**	be**lt**	restaura**nt**	fir**st**	sa**nd**

7 — CHAT TIME

1. Have you ever been involved in an accident of any kind?
2. Have you ever broken a bone or had stitches for a cut or wound?
3. Do you think some people have more accidents than others? Why or why not?
4. What are the most common kinds of accidents among people you know?

8 CONVERSATION

ACCIDENTS HAPPEN

Mark: So how did you hurt yourself?
Selma: I didn't use mitts while I was taking the roast out of the oven, so I burned myself.
Mark: So did I. I was making fries, and some hot oil splashed on me.
I keep having accidents all the time.
Selma: So do I. I've had accidents all my life.
Mark: So have I. I've had all types of accidents since I was a kid. I fell down the stairs on my tricycle, and I had to have stitches on my forehead. Another time I drank antiseptic thinking it was soda, and I was really sick.
The doctors and nurses at the local hospital all knew me.
Selma: Well, I remember being run over by a cyclist as a little girl. Once I dove into the low end of a swimming pool and hit my head. Once I slipped when I was stepping off a curb, and I sprained my ankle. And recently I got my hair caught in the hairdryer and some of it got burned.
I wonder what people like us should do.

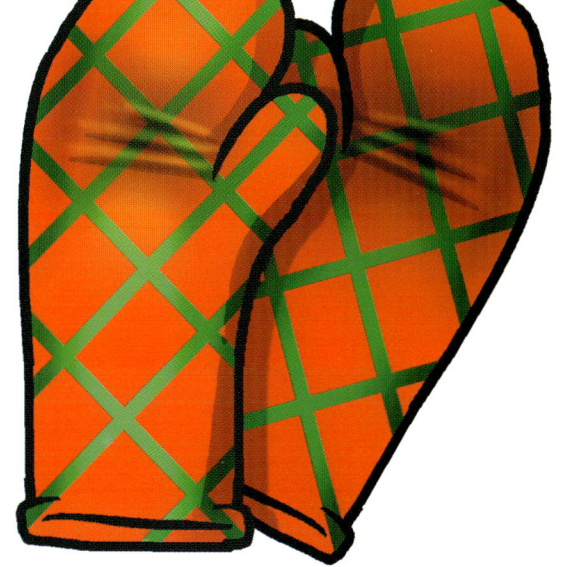

YOUR ENDING
What advice do you think Mark gives Selma?
① We need to have a good health plan.
② We should be more careful.
③ We have to try doing things more slowly.
④ Your idea: _____

ABOUT THE CONVERSATION
1. What's wrong with Mark and Selma?
2. What accidents have they had in the past?
3. Why did the doctors and nurses know Mark?

9 YOUR TURN

A Act out the conversation with a partner. Use these prompts.

| Selma's current problem | Mark's accidents: tricycle, antiseptic |
| Mark's current problem | Selma's accidents: cyclist, swimming pool, curb, hairdryer |

B Imagine you are Mark or Selma. Relate one of your accidents in detail to the class.

Example:
It happened while I was crossing the street.
I was looking up and trying to see the clock on the department store . . .

10 — READING

BEFORE READING
Have you ever heard or read about unusual accidents or deaths? What do you remember about them?

> **READING**
> Articles are often broken into sections with subheadings. The subheadings give information about changes in topics. Read them carefully.

Unusual Accidents and Deaths

We often wonder how people actually survived accidents or about the unusual circumstances in which people were killed. Here are some really amazing stories—some from history and then one firsthand from a local citizen.

Unhappy Endings
According to legend, the ancient Greek playwright Aeschylus was killed when an eagle dropped a tortoise on his head. The bird was trying to break the tortoise's shell on a rock in order to eat it. Aeschylus was bald, and the eagle thought the unfortunate man's head was a good rock for breaking a turtle.

On Memorial Day of 1987, a forty-year-old Louisiana lawyer was in his boat as a thunderstorm approached. He raised his arms over his head to the sky and said, as if to challenge nature: "Here I am." He was struck by a bolt of lightning and died instantly. The man's first name was Graves.

Some people worry about being hit from things falling from outer space. There is only one person in all recorded history who has been killed by a meteorite—Manfredo Settala (1600-1680).

Happy Endings
A German soldier was riding in the back seat of a World War I plane when the engine suddenly stopped. He fell out of his seat while the plane was over two miles above ground. As he was falling, the plane started falling too, and he was blown back into his own seat by the wind. The pilot was able to land the plane safely.

Bob Hail jumped out of an airplane. His main parachute failed. His backup parachute also failed. He hit the ground face first. After a moment, he got up and walked away with only minor injuries.

And now a true-life story from a local citizen . . .

The following is an interview with Ricardo Lima, who fell from the fourth floor of a building when he was two years old—and survived.

Reporter: How on earth did you fall out of the window?
Ricardo: I was pretty mischievous when I was a kid. I was always up to something.
Reporter: Were you alone when it happened?
Ricardo: No. I was sitting with my mother in the living room playing with my toys. My sister started crying in the bedroom, and my mom went to take care of her. So I pushed a chair near a window and climbed on top to have a look outside.
Reporter: You can't let kids out of your sight for a second.
Ricardo: Yeah. And while I was leaning on the windowsill, my pacifier fell out of my mouth. I tried to grab it, and I lost my balance and fell.
Reporter: My goodness! And do you remember the fall?
Ricardo: It was all very quick, but I remember lying on the ground with people all around me. And then I saw my mom. She was desperate, because she thought I was dead, but all I had was a broken leg. I was very lucky. I might have died.
Reporter: That's for sure. But I heard you first hit an awning, and that helped to break your fall. Is that right?
Ricardo: No. I fell right onto a concrete sidewalk. Tough folks can fall onto concrete—and survive, I guess!

> "Tough folks can fall onto concrete—and survive, I guess!"

AFTER READING

A Answer *true* or *false*.

1. ___ The bird thought that Aeschylus' head was a tortoise.
2. ___ Graves died because his boat overturned.
3. ___ It is common for people to be hit by meteorites.
4. ___ The pilot fell out of his seat but was blown back into it by the wind.
5. ___ Bob Hail's first parachute failed, so his backup parachute saved him.

B Summarize Ricardo's story.

DISCUSSION

1. Which incident do you think is the strangest or the most interesting? Why?
2. Irony occurs when something that is unexpected happens.
   What is the irony in the story about the man in the boat?
3. Do you know of anyone who almost died or was injured in an accident? What happened?
4. Why do you think people are interested in stories of other people's disasters?

11 — WRITING

Write about an accident you had or witnessed.

> *It happened when I was ten years old. I was climbing our neighbor's peach tree...*

12 — PROJECT

> - *Choose an area that has a lot of accidents (specific sports, jobs, etc.).*
> - *Prepare a prevention campaign for it and write a set of rules.*
>   *Present your campaign to the class.*

6 TAKE MY ADVICE

LOOK AND LISTEN

HELP 4 U
http://www.help4u.com

You've got questions?   **We've got the answers.**

| Dating | Divorce | Drugs | Eating | Friends | Relationships | School/College |

This site has been developed to help people who have problems and don't know who to turn to for help. We hope you will use it and make the right choices in your life!

Saying NO to drugs

You want to stay healthy? Then you'd better stay away from drugs. Turn them down!

The term *drug* refers to dangerous and illegal substances, including alcohol and tobacco. Drugs affect people of all ages and classes.

You should keep your principles and your sense of self-worth.

In case of peer pressure, just say NO!

(For help with any drug-related problems, call 1-555-NO-DRUGS or 663-7847. We have experienced counselors available day and night.)

Weight Control

I HAVE TO LOSE WEIGHT. WHAT SHOULD I DO?

YOU'D BETTER GAIN WEIGHT. YOU'RE TOO THIN.

Anorexia

Anorexia is an eating disorder that affects people's appetite—usually because of emotional problems. This condition is quite common among teenage girls between the ages of 13 and 18, but it can also be found in boys. Many young people dream of becoming top models. The slim look is usually considered desirable. Therefore, in order to keep their weight down, these young people simply avoid food.

Keeping Fit

Fitness means "being in good physical condition—healthy and strong" and is usually associated with exercise. That is not the whole picture. In order to keep fit, you have to eat well, sleep well, and generally feel good about yourself.

WHAT SHOULD I DO TO BE LIKE YOU?

YOU OUGHT TO EAT HEALTHY FOOD, AND YOU COULD TAKE UP A SPORT.

YEAH. I KEEP PUTTING IT OFF.

Dating

Some tips on dating.

- You should avoid people who—
  - think their partner is a possession
  - are extremely jealous
  - try to control you
  - abuse drugs and alcohol
  - change their mood suddenly
  - always have to have their way
- Go out in couples, with friends who can help you in case of trouble.
- You ought to stay in public places, especially for the first few dates.
- Try to carry a cell phone so that you can call for help anytime or if you want to leave early.
- You might take a self-defense class, such as karate.

1 — COMPREHENSION

1. Who should you call in case of drug addiction?
2. What should you do if you're too thin?
3. Why do some young people avoid food?
4. What might you do in order to stay fit?
5. What should people do to stay safe on a date?

EMERGENCY CALL

2 — PAIR WORK

A Ask and give advice about the problems on these pages and similar problems.

- What should I do to lose weight?
- You ought to exercise, and you shouldn't eat a lot of junk food.

- I'm feeling depressed, and I don't know why.
- You'd better see a doctor.

B What are the three most common problems for people you know? Write them down. Compare your list with a partner's. Share advice for people who have the problems.

3 GRAMMAR

Modal auxiliaries: *should, ought to, might, could*

Use **should, ought to, might** and **could** to give advice.

Question (?)	Affirmative (+)	Negative (-)
Should I stay or should I go?	You should stay.	You shouldn't go.
	You ought to stay.	You ought not to stay.
	You might stay.	
	You could stay.	

Note: **Ought to** is stronger than **should**.
Might and **could** are less strong than **ought to** and **should**.

Had better

Had better is also used to give advice. It is stronger than **should** and **ought to**.

Question (?)	Affirmative (+)	Negative (-)
Should I take this medicine?	You'd better take it.	You'd better not take it.

Two- and three-word verbs

The meaning of two- and three-word verbs is often very different from the words taken separately.

1. Verb + adverb participle
   - to **put** something **off** (postpone) — They **put off** the meeting till next week.
   - to **give** something **up** (stop doing) — She **gave up** smoking when the baby was born.
   - to **take** something **up** (begin) — I'm going to **take up** the guitar.
   - to **throw** something **away** (discard) — Don't **throw away** your old clothes.
   - to **turn** something **down** (refuse) — The company **turned down** my offer.
   - to **turn to** someone ask for help — People often **turn to** their families in bad times.

2. Verb + adverb participle + preposition
   - to **break up with** someone (stop dating) — John **broke up with** his girlfriend.
   - to **get along with** someone (be friendly) — Carol and I **get along** well **with** each other.
   - to **put up with** someone or something (accept a bad situation) — My boss is difficult to **put up with**.

Note: Pronoun objects go between the verb and particle: I can't find my old sneakers. Did you throw **them** away?

Infinitive of purpose with **in order to**

Use **to** or **in order to** to talk about the reasons you do things.

I took up a sport **(in order) to** keep fit and healthy.

So and **therefore**

Use **so** and **therefore** to express logical consequences or results.

Sally has a skin problem, **so** she went to a dermatologist.
Some people want to lose weight; **therefore**, they drink diet sodas.

A Substitute the words in parentheses with two-word and three-word verbs. You may have to add pronouns.

1. Thank you for your offer, but I'm going to have to _____ (refuse) your help.
2. I cleaned up my closet and _____ (discard) a lot of old clothes.
3. We have nowhere to stay. Can you _____ (accommodate)?
4. Charles is in financial difficulties, but he has no one to _____ (ask for help).
5. I have to finish my big report. Can we _____ (postpone) our date?
6. Samuel wants to lose weight. He ought to _____ (begin) a sport like jogging. He should also _____ (stop) eating sweets.
7. Mei's boyfriend is very jealous, and she wants _____ (stop dating).
8. I have a new person who shares my apartment. Unfortunately we _____ (not have a good relationship). I have to _____ (accept) his messy ways.

B Give advice. What would you say in the following situations?

> Example:
> A friend is traveling by car in a foreign country.
> He/She doesn't know the roads very well.
>
> You'd better take a bilingual road map in case you get lost.

1. A friend has just broken up with his/her boyfriend/girlfriend.
2. A friend is looking for a boyfriend/girlfriend. Where can he/she go to meet people?
3. A friend's parents are getting a divorce. What do you say to him/her to help cope?
4. A friend is trying to give up smoking.
5. A friend wants to lose weight.
6. A friend has very low self-esteem.
7. A friend is feeling down and depressed.
8. A friend is going out on a date with someone for the first time.

C Combine the following sentences using *in order to, so,* or *therefore*.

1. Depression affects people of all ages. If you feel sad, go see a doctor. (*so*)
2. You need to buy this medicine. You need a prescription. (*in order to*)
3. Julie stayed away from classes for a month. She needs to catch up. (*therefore*)
4. Hank spends all his time on the Internet. His grades are bad. (*therefore*)
5. Mary found out her boyfriend was cheating on her. She broke up the relationship. (*so*)
6. You must say a definite no to drugs. You want to stay healthy. (*in order to*)
7. My friends were drinking at the party. I decided not to get into the car with them. (*so*)
8. Ted always drank soda and only ate junk food. He put on a lot of weight. (*therefore*)

4 — GRAMMAR TALK

A With a partner, make as many two-word and three-word verbs as you can with the verbs below. You need to add particles such as *up, down, out, away, in, off*. Write sentences with the verbs. Use a dictionary to help you.

break	_____	look	_____
come	_____	put	_____
get	_____	take	_____
give	_____	turn	_____

B Read your sentences in small groups. Can the other students guess the meanings of the verbs?

5 — LISTENING

Three teenagers are talking to Dr. Wise about their problems. Complete the chart.

	Problem	Doctor's advice
Harvey		
Cindy		
Mike		

6 — PRONUNCIATION

Listen and practice. The main stress is on second part of the two-word or three-word verb.

put **off**	I **put off** my new diet.
break **up** with	Linda has **broken up with** her boyfriend.
turn **down**	I don't want to **turn down** a friend who asks for help.

7 — CHAT TIME

1. What people do you get along well with?
   Do you have special friends?
   Are you close to members of your family?
2. Name some people that are easy/difficult to get along with.
3. Do you have friends who are into drugs? How can you help?
4. Do you know anyone who suffers from anorexia?
5. Are you weight conscious?
6. Are you concerned about your health and fitness?
7. What kind of diseases are common among people you know?
8. When was the last time you were ill?

8 — CONVERSATION

John: Hey, Mary, you look depressed. Is everything OK?
Mary: It's my parents. They're not easy to put up with. They're so old-fashioned, and they never let me do anything. I go out at night only once in a while, and when I do, I have to be back by twelve. What should I do?
John: Have you tried to talk to them?
Mary: They never have any time for me. My dad's work comes first, and my mom only sits down with me when she wants to show me off to her friends: "Mary gets straight As, and she made the basketball team this year." Ugh! I want to move out and live on my own.
John: Well, I get along well with my parents, but we don't agree all the time. They worry too much about me. If I'm going away, it's always: "Don't forget to call as soon as you arrive. Take this medicine with you in case you get sick. You must stay away from drugs." They know I'm not into that! They should trust me.
Mary: I guess parents are all the same.

ABOUT THE CONVERSATION

1. What's Mary's problem with her parents? What don't they let her do?
2. What's Mary's relationship with her mom and dad?
3. What's John's problem with his parents?
4. Do you think parents are all the same? Why?

9 — YOUR TURN

A Act out the conversation with a partner. Use the following prompts.

John: Look/depressed
Mary: Parents/old-fashioned/don't let me do things
John: Tried to talk with them?
Mary: No time for me
John: Get along with parents/worry too much

B Pretend Mary has asked for your advice. What do you say?
Work with a partner. Present your conversation to the class.

10 — READING

BEFORE READING
1. Write down what you think are the main ingredients for a good relationship.
2. List the factors that normally lead people to break up a relationship.

BREAKING UP—BROKEN HEARTS

A good relationship is built on honesty, trust, and mutual respect. Some relationships can last a very long time. Other relationships can go downhill fast or so slowly you don't realize how bad they have gotten. Now, when do you know it's time to break up?

The following is a checklist to help you determine when it's time to move on. Just ONE "warning sign" is enough reason to break up.

- You shouldn't put up with an abusive partner. There is never an acceptable excuse for a partner to hurt you with words or actions. You don't have to tolerate any verbal or physical abuse. You should not accept common excuses like "I just had a bad day at work!," "I'm under a lot of stress!," "I'm really sorry. I promise I won't do it again!" You should think carefully before giving a person a second chance.
- Your partner should respect your opinions, decisions, morals, and values. He or she should support you and encourage you to reach your goals and dreams.
- If your partner has a problem with alcohol or drugs, you had better not believe that you'll be able to change his or her ways.
- You ought to have time for yourself, your family, and your friends. Your partner shouldn't be possessive and take up all your time and energy.
- If you can't trust your partner, if you think that he/she lies or cheats, or if he/she makes you feel unsafe, then you'd better listen to your instincts.
- If you no longer enjoy time together, if you don't respect each other, or if you can't be honest with each other, then it's better to be on your own than in a bad relationship.

But breaking up can leave you feeling down. Don't worry, this happens all the time, and it shouldn't last too long. Here is some advice on getting over a broken heart.

- You ought to spend some time on your own in order to examine your feelings, but you mustn't become a hermit.
- You should turn off the TV, and keep busy doing the things you enjoy.
- Get out of the house and spend time with your friends.
- Remind yourself of your good qualities. Make a list!
- You should treat yourself right: get enough sleep, eat right (stay away from junk food and caffeine), and spend a little extra time on how you look.
- Most important: Don't feel sorry for yourself. Accept what happened and move on.

AFTER READING

A Answer *true* or *false* according to the information in the article.

1. _____ Some relationships get bad very slowly over time.
2. _____ Studies show that partners can usually change each other's habits.
3. _____ If you don't trust your partner, it might be time to break up.
4. _____ If you break up, you should immediately try to get a new boyfriend/girlfriend.

B Complete the following sentences based on the reading.

1. A good relationship should have _____.
2. "I'm under a lot of pressure" shouldn't be an excuse for _____.
3. Your partner should encourage you to _____.
4. If you don't trust each other anymore, then you'd better _____.
5. Breaking up happens all the time; therefore, you shouldn't _____.

DISCUSSION

1. Do you think there are other reasons for breaking up?
2. Do you agree with the advice in the reading?
3. Have you ever broken up with someone? What helped you get over it?
4. What advice can you give someone who is suffering from a broken heart?

11 — WRITING

Look through advice columns in magazines, newspapers, or on the Web or in other places where people write about their problems. Choose one common problem that interests you and write your personal advice about the problem in general.

12 — PROJECT

- Research community resources that provide people help with various kinds of problems.
- Investigate one and present it to the class.

EXPANSION 2

1 — READING

BEFORE READING
What do you know about stress? Discuss with a partner.

teenage stress

Definition
Stress - the mental and physical strain or the non-specific response of the body to any demand made upon it. Stress is a chemical reaction that takes place inside the body when there is a basic need to adapt to or resist changing internal or external influences. It is a response meant to return the body and mind to a state of equilibrium and balance.

The Causes of Stress

Although adolescence is often viewed by parents as a carefree period of life, some studies show that teenagers experience the most stress of all people. They can experience stress related to money, family problems, self-esteem, acceptance by their peers, getting accepted into college, choosing a career, and pressure to do well in school, sports, or clubs.

According to experts, one of the main reasons for stress is that childhood has gotten shorter, and the perception of children has changed. Since TV is available to any audience, children can get messages that were probably meant for adults, and the dividing line between childhood and adulthood ceases to exist. Children do not play as many of their own games as they used to, and most of their games and sports nowadays are those preferred by adults. Youngsters wear similar clothing to that of adults, and they use adult language that was once never to be heard around a child. Young people these days are under tremendous pressure to achieve, please, and succeed. They are expected to adjust to social environmental changes that past generations never had to deal with. The demands made on preteens and teens by modern life have definitely increased the level of stress.

54

Tips for Dealing with Stress

All humans experience stress. It is a necessary part of life. The response to stress is what often needs to be controlled. A person's feelings, attitudes, and outlook on life affect his or her ability to deal with stress.

⭐ You should avoid unnecessary worry. Thinking about a problem in order to arrive at a solution can be positive, but constant worry that is not constructive accomplishes nothing. It usually just makes situations more stressful.

⭐ Become better organized. Plan activities a step at a time so that parts are accomplished. This gives you more self-esteem and more reasonable deadlines.

⭐ You should be aware of the symptoms of stress. Some symptoms are:
- moodiness;
- insomnia or other sleeping disorders;
- lowered body resistance to colds, flu, or other diseases;
- preoccupation with negative/angry thoughts or feelings;
- unusual behavior patterns; and
- loss of appetite, or eating disorders such as anorexia or bulimia.

⭐ When you know you have a problem with stress, try to solve it one step at a time. Part of the problem could be trying to do too much at once. You should take it in easy stages.

Conclusion

Stress doesn't need to be negative. Some doctors say that you should laugh and smile more frequently. When you laugh and smile, your body relaxes, and it causes a positive reaction.

AFTER READING

A Which of the following is the writer doing in the text? Mark your answers.
1. ____ expressing an opinion
2. ____ giving advice
3. ____ giving the solutions for stress
4. ____ telling readers how to cope with stress
5. ____ getting people to do things
6. ____ talking about cause and effect

B Answer about the text.
1. List the causes of stress.
2. Why is stress more common nowadays than in the past?
3. What should you do about it?

2 — WRITING

Write about the things that cause stress in your age group.

3 ACTIVITIES

A Read about Sally's lifestyle. Do you think she suffers from stress? Give advice, using *should*, *ought to*, *had better*, or *must*.

- works 8–9 hours a day in the office
- takes work to do at home
- drinks a lot of coffee
- spends an hour and a half in traffic
- doesn't have time to exercise
- rarely goes out with friends
- does all the house chores herself
- hasn't had a vacation in two years

B Complete the questionnaire. Compare your answers with a partner and discuss solutions.

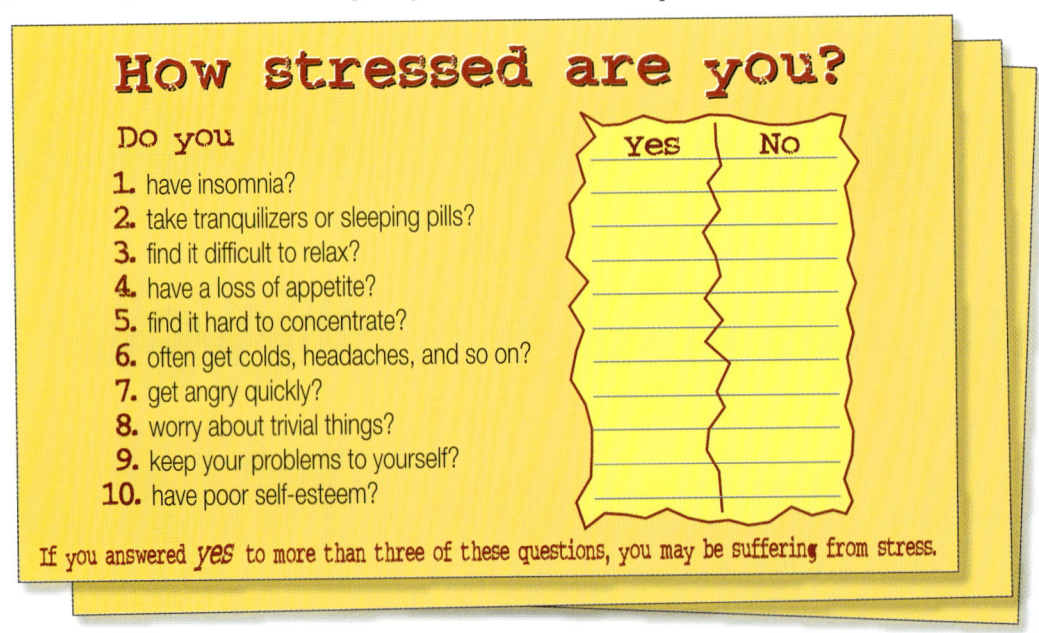

How stressed are you?

Do you

	Yes	No
1. have insomnia?		
2. take tranquilizers or sleeping pills?		
3. find it difficult to relax?		
4. have a loss of appetite?		
5. find it hard to concentrate?		
6. often get colds, headaches, and so on?		
7. get angry quickly?		
8. worry about trivial things?		
9. keep your problems to yourself?		
10. have poor self-esteem?		

If you answered *yes* to more than three of these questions, you may be suffering from stress.

C Complete the ad, using the correct form of each word in parentheses.

Paradise Resort
Hotel and Spa

The (good) _____ solution to fitness of mind and body

A world of grandeur awaits you at one of the (exclusive) _____ spa resorts in the Caribbean. This award-winning resort (locate) _____ on Paradise Island and (build) _____ only recently. The spa has a unique setting and offers guests a wide choice of magnificently (decorate) _____ bedrooms or villas (surround) _____ by palm trees. Exquisite gourmet dishes (prepare) _____ by international chefs. Our staff is dedicated to (meet) _____ your every need. So prepare to pamper yourself and emerge renewed.

Fitness Facilities and Services

Spa Paradise focuses on the exotic and blends the (fine) _____ healing techniques from cultures around the globe.

Nutritional Consultation

In order to benefit from a complete fitness program, (allow) _____ one of our nutritionists to create a healthy diet for you.

Stress Management

Learn techniques to change your attitude and actions. You should (transform) _____ stress into creative opportunities. Improve concentration, memory, stress reduction, and peace of mind.

Personal Fitness Training

A program to develop your endurance, strength, and flexibility for your mind and body can (design) _____ by our highly qualified fitness experts.

The Games Court

This indoor, air-conditioned court (be) _____ available to all guests. You may (reserve) _____ court time for a private lesson or challenge our pro. All necessary equipment (provide) _____ by the hotel at no charge.

4 — TALK ABOUT IT

1. Are there spas in your country? What are they like?
2. Have you ever been to a spa? Do you know anyone who has?

7 DEAR FRIENDS

LOOK AND LISTEN

Treetop Lumber Inc.
824 Elm Road
June 15

Dear Mr. Gonzalez:

I want to apologize for not answering your letter sooner. I've been out of the office for the last three weeks, and I only got back yesterday.

Although the focus of our company is on the U.S market, we are very interested in expanding into Latin America. I look forward to meeting you and discussing the various possibilities. Please give me a call as soon as you arrive on March 29, so that we can set up a time for a meeting.

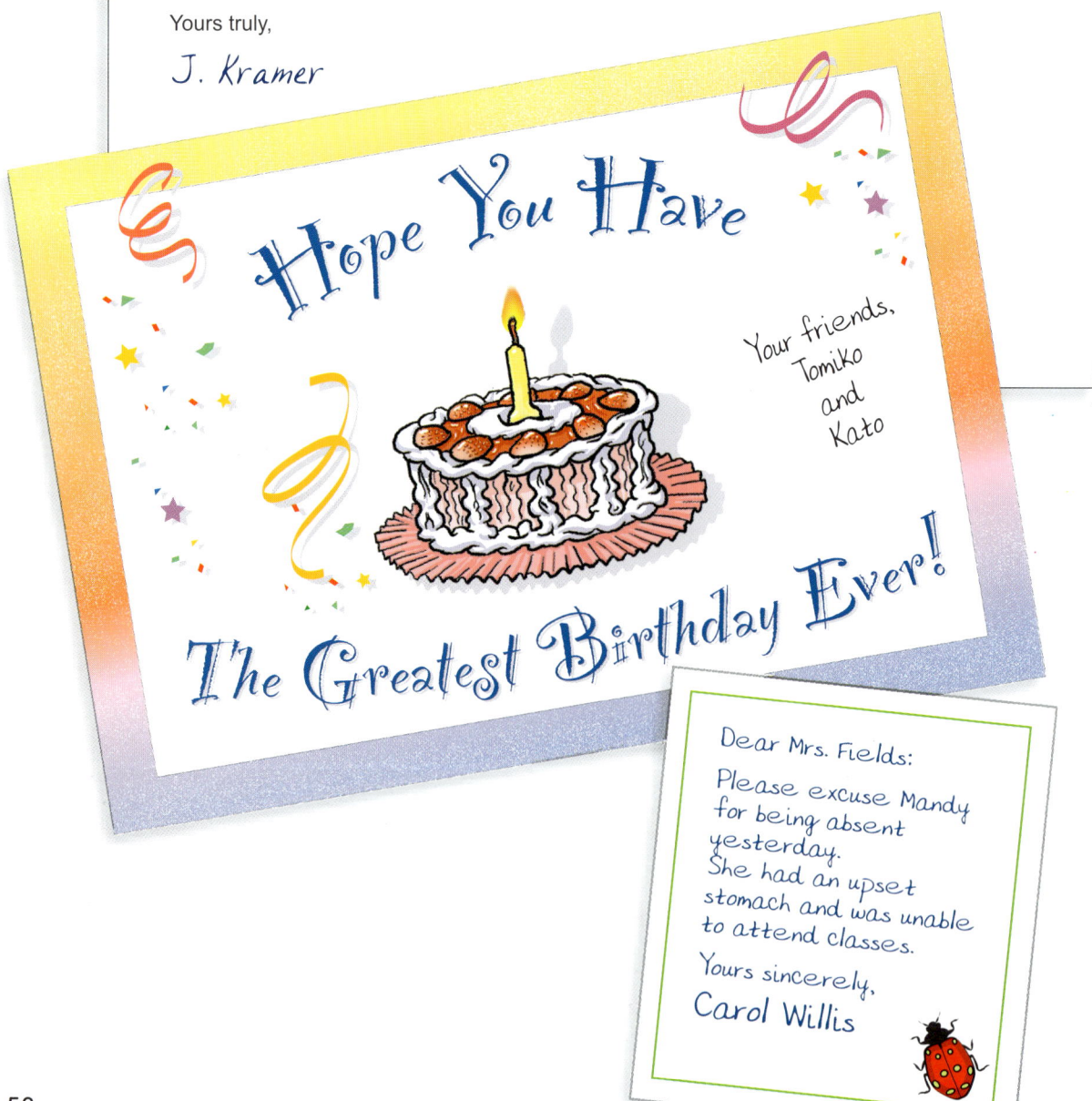

Yours truly,

J. Kramer

Hope You Have The Greatest Birthday Ever!

Your friends,
Tomiko
and
Kato

Dear Mrs. Fields:

Please excuse Mandy for being absent yesterday. She had an upset stomach and was unable to attend classes.

Yours sincerely,
Carol Willis

ROD'S 19th BIRTHDAY PARTY

Saturday, November 25
Meet at the bowling alley
@ 9:00 P.M. sharp!

419 Brunswick Avenue
Richmond

(234) 567-3891
Please RSVP by November 12

March 15

Dear Liz,

I'm writing to ask you a favor. I tried calling you, but your number has changed.

I'm coming to New York at the end of the month to go to a conference. Can you let me stay for a couple of days? I'm used to sleeping anywhere. Please let me know if this is all right.

What's the weather like now? Last time I was in New York it was so cold that I almost froze, in spite of all the clothing I had on.

Love,
Brenda

P.S. I'm mailing this to your office, because last time we talked you told me that you were going to move to a new apartment.

GET WELL SOON

Glad to hear that you're getting better.

Love,
Michael

---

1 — COMPREHENSION

Answer *true* or *false*.
1. ____ Mr. Kramer didn't write sooner because he was away.
2. ____ Mr. Kramer is not interested in meeting Mr. Gonzalez.
3. ____ Mandy went to school in spite of her upset stomach.
4. ____ Rod's friends need to confirm if they are coming to the party.
5. ____ Tomiko and Kato are congratulating a friend for passing his/her exams.
6. ____ Brenda wants to stay with Liz.

2 — PAIR WORK

A Apologize for something.

- I want to apologize for not coming to your party.
- Don't worry. That's quite all right.

B Wish someone the best on a special occasion.

- I wish you lots of success in your new position.
- Thanks a lot. I'm looking forward to the new job.

C Ask and refuse a favor.

- Can you put us up for the night?
- I'm afraid I can't. I already have someone staying with me.

D Write down what you're used to/not used to doing on special occasions and holidays and compare with your partner.

- I'm not used to receiving cards on my birthday.
- Neither am I.

3 — GRAMMAR

Preposition + gerund

In English, gerund forms follow prepositions.

We talked **about going** to New York for vacation.

Some verbs are usually followed by certain prepositions.

excuse (someone) for doing	Please excuse Mary for being absent.
apologize for doing	I apologize for not coming to the reception.
look forward to doing	I'm looking forward to lying in the sun.
think of doing	I'm thinking of moving to a new apartment soon.

Some verbs are usually followed by certain prepositions.

used to doing	I'm used to working hard.
tired of doing	I'm tired of waiting.

Future in the past

Use future in the past to talk about something that had not yet happened at the time.

Last time **I saw** you, you **were going to start** a new job.

Although vs. in spite of

In spite of and *although* have similar meanings. **In spite of** is followed by a noun or gerund. *Although* introduces a clause that has a subject and verb.

The letter arrived **in spite of** the incorrect address./He went to school **in spite of** being sick.
Although the letter was addressed incorrectly, I received it.

Adverbs of degree: *so . . . that*

Use *so* with an adjective or with **many, much, few,** or *little* to express result.

The noise was **so loud** (that) we were hardly able to hear ourselves talk.
There were **so many** people (that) we couldn't find a place to sit.

Can—could

Present
It is so hot (that) we **can't** sleep.

Past
It was so hot (that) we **couldn't** sleep.

Clauses of time: *as soon as, when*

Conjunctions of time are not followed by the future. Use the present or past instead.

I'll tell you **as soon as I know.**   I'll call you **when I arrive.**

A Match the following sentences. Mary is telling a friend about an outing.
1. ____ There was so much traffic on the road
2. ____ The picnic spot was so crowded
3. ____ The water was so cold
4. ____ There were so many mosquitoes
5. ____ I was so upset that
6. ____ We were all so tired in the evening

a. we couldn't swim.
b. it took us hours to get to the beach.
c. we went straight to bed.
d. I wanted to cry.
e. we couldn't find a place to park.
f. the children were bitten all over.

B Use the following words to complete the text:

although, as soon as, because, but, during, in spite of.

The Singing Telegram

_____ the Depression in 1933, many people were out of work. It was that year in which George Oslin, a Western Union executive, invented history's first singing telegram. To a lot of people after World War I, a telegram was a scary thing _____ it meant you were being informed that you lost a loved one. When Oslin presented his idea to his bosses, he was told that his idea was a bad one. But he fought for his idea _____ the opposition of his bosses.
_____ the singing telegram was started, it became wildly popular with the U.S. public. _____ Western Union made millions of dollars with his idea, Mr. Oslin didn't die a rich man. Today singing telegrams aren't used anymore, _____ you can still send one over the telephone, to the tune of "Happy Birthday," at a cost of about $17.

"HAPPY BIRTHDAY, MY DARLING. MANY HAPPY RETURNS. I LONG FOR YOU, I YEARN FOR YOU, YOU KNOW MY HEART BURNS."

C Complete the sentences about yourself.
Then compare with a partner.

Example: I'm thinking of *working in a foreign country.*
1. I'm interested in _____
2. I'm excited about _____
3. I'm thinking of _____
4. I'm looking forward to _____
5. I'm not used to _____
6. I'm tired of _____
7. I apologized to my friend for _____
8. I'm not capable of _____

4 — GRAMMAR TALK

Make a list of things you're **used to doing** and **not used to doing** and compare with a partner.

Example:
I'm used to studying with other people.
I'm not used to driving in the snow.

Possibilities
getting up early,
working hard,
eating spicy food,
being by myself a lot, etc.

5 — LISTENING

A Listen to the four people. Answer *true* or *false*.
1. _____ Mr. Kramer wants to put off the meeting with Mr. Gonzalez.
2. _____ Liz is thinking of letting her friend stay with her.
3. _____ At first, Mike plans to go to Rod's party in spite of the visit from his relatives.
4. _____ Although Rod was sick, he was able to finish the project.

B Listen again. Complete the sentences.
1. Mr. Kramer is thinking of _____.
2. Although Liz's apartment is small, _____.
3. Mike is looking forward to _____.
4. Raymond was so sick that _____.

6 — PRONUNCIATION

Listen and practice. The following are sometimes called short vowels.

Friend.
F-R-I-E-N-D.

Expand.
E-X-P-A-N-D.

/ɛ/	/æ/	/ɪ/
friend	absent	sincerely
send	expand	interested

The sound /ɛ/ is usually spelled with the letter e. Another common spelling is *ea (head)*.
The sound /æ/ is usually spelled with the letter a.
The sound /ɪ/ is usually spelled with the letter i. It is sometimes spelled with *y (gym)* or *e (English)*.

7 — CHAT TIME

1. Are people in your country used to writing notes, letters, or cards on special occasions?
2. Do you apologize for not doing something or doing something wrong?
   When did you last apologize? Was it easy or hard for you?
3. Are you the kind of person who forgives easily?
4. When you are absent from school, do your parents have to write notes explaining your absence?
5. Do you like doing favors or asking other people for favors?

8 — CONVERSATION

GREAT IDEAS

Linda: Rod, thanks for inviting me to your party, but I'm not going to be able to make it.
Rod: Why not?
Linda: Well, you see, my cousin is getting engaged. It's one of those family parties, and I have to go. I'd prefer to come to your party instead, but you know how it is. I don't want to let the family down.
Rod: That's a real shame. We're going to miss you.

* * *

Tony: Hey, Rod, thanks for the invitation. I think it's a really cool idea to have a birthday party in a bowling alley.
Rod: Yeah. At first, I was going to have it in a club, but then I changed my mind.
Tony: This is much more fun. Millie had her birthday at Dancin' Nights, and it was so loud we couldn't talk, and it was too crowded. You always come up with great ideas.

YOUR ENDING

What do you think Rod says next?
① Next year I'm thinking of having my birthday party in a stretch limo.
② Wait till next year. I have a whole year to think of something great!
③ Thanks. I'm simply brilliant, don't you think?
④ Your idea: _____

ABOUT THE CONVERSATION
1. Why is Rod having a party?
2. Why can't Linda come to the party?
3. Why isn't Rod having his party at the club?

9 — YOUR TURN

A Do a role play with a partner.
You can't come to your friend's party.
Make up a reason. Apologize for not coming.

B Do the following role play: Call a friend and accept an invitation to a party.

C Do the following role play with a partner: Plan a birthday party in an unusual place. Call and invite a friend.

63

10 READING

BEFORE READING

List the different forms of communication you know. Compare and discuss with a partner.

READING

Very often writers use examples to show their ideas. What examples of communicating do you find in the reading? Why does the author include them?

FROM SMOKE SIGNALS TO E-MAIL
Keeping in touch

From the Stone Age to the present, people have shown a definite need to send messages to one another despite being far away.

In 1084 B.C., a chain of fires on mountaintops was used to relate the news of the fall of Troy to people in Greece. In the past, native people in the Americas used smoke from fires to transmit messages. They developed a code—in which certain combinations had special meanings. For example, two parallel columns of smoke indicated the successful return of a war party.

Almost anything that makes a noise has been used for signaling. Cyrus, an ancient Persian ruler, established lines of signal towers. At each one, people with powerful voices shouted a message to the next tower. A kind of drum talk is still used in Central Africa today, although few who are not natives have been able to understand it. The sender uses a drum that can produce a high or low tone. Because the local dialect alternates in these tones, the sender is able to simulate speech with the drums.

In modern times, people have communicated by letter, telegraph, and telephone. But no one method has become as widespread as quickly as the use of e-mail.

In 1990, the number of people on e-mail was small, but by the end of the twentieth century, there were 263 million e-mail boxes, and in the United States alone, 9.3 million messages were sent a day. And e-mail use is expected to increase by 15 to 25 percent a year.

The first e-mail message took place in 1971, and according to its sender, Ray Tomlinson, it was probably the following: "QWERTYUIOP." What was significant about that? Nothing, really. This is just the top row of keys on an English-language keyboard. Tomlinson was just testing out an idea. He had no concept that he was going to start a revolution in communication.

Tomlinson was one of a group of scientists who were working on developing better computers. The scientists at his site were able to send a message to a "mailbox" on the computer on their site. Other scientists could view the messages in the mailbox. But there were other computers at other sites where scientists were working on the same project. Tomlinson's idea was to figure out a way to deliver messages to mailboxes on those remote computers. He used the @ sign to identify messages that were headed out of the local machine to the more distant ones. And the rest is history.

The Internet has become so popular nowadays that when you ask someone his or her address, the answer might be JSmith@net.com instead of 123 King Street.

AFTER READING

Complete the following sentences about the reading.

1. People have shown a need to keep in touch with one another by _____.
2. When Native Americans saw two columns of smoke, _____.
3. In central Africa, the tone of the drums is so specific that natives _____.
4. Although e-mail only began in the 1970s, by the end of the century _____.
5. When Tomlinson sent his first message, he had no idea _____.
6. Nowadays millions of people are used to _____.

DISCUSSION

1. What are the most common ways that you communicate with friends? With relatives? With people who live far away?
2. What are the advantages and disadvantages of the various ways of communicating?

11 — WRITING

Write a letter or e-mail to a friend telling some good/bad news.

Dear Jennifer, (letter) or Hi, Jennifer, (e-mail)

I have to share the news with a good friend. You'll never imagine what happened ...

12 — PROJECT

- *Write and design cards for special occasions. You can use a computer to make your cards, or make them by hand.*
- *Present your cards to the class.*

8 WISHFUL THINKING

LOOK AND LISTEN

WHAT PEOPLE ARE SAYING

Wishes vary from person to person.
Find out what some of our readers answered to the following questions, and why.

If you could take only one thing with you to a desert island, what would you take?
I would take my cell phone. I'd be able to talk to my friends and wouldn't get lonely.
Angela, age 23

If you had a close encounter with an extraterrestrial, what question would you ask?
I'd ask the creature if I could travel with him or her. I would like to find out about life in the universe.
Tony, age 25

If you could go anywhere, where would you go and why?
I'd go to the South Pole, because I live in Egypt, and I've never seen the snow.
Ahmed, age 18

If you could choose a place to live, which city or country would you choose?
If I could choose a place to live, I'd go to Hawaii. The weather's great the whole year round, and the surfing is fabulous.
Mike, age 17

If you could be an animal, what animal would you be?
I would be a dolphin because dolphins are intelligent creatures, and they have lots of fun.
Yoko, age 15

If you could be a historical figure, who would you be?
I'd be Marie Antoinette and live in the luxury of Versailles. But I wouldn't want to go to the guillotine.
Dianne, age 21

If you could travel through time, would you go the past or to the future?
I would go to the future to see what I'd look like as an adult.
Marie Claire, age 12

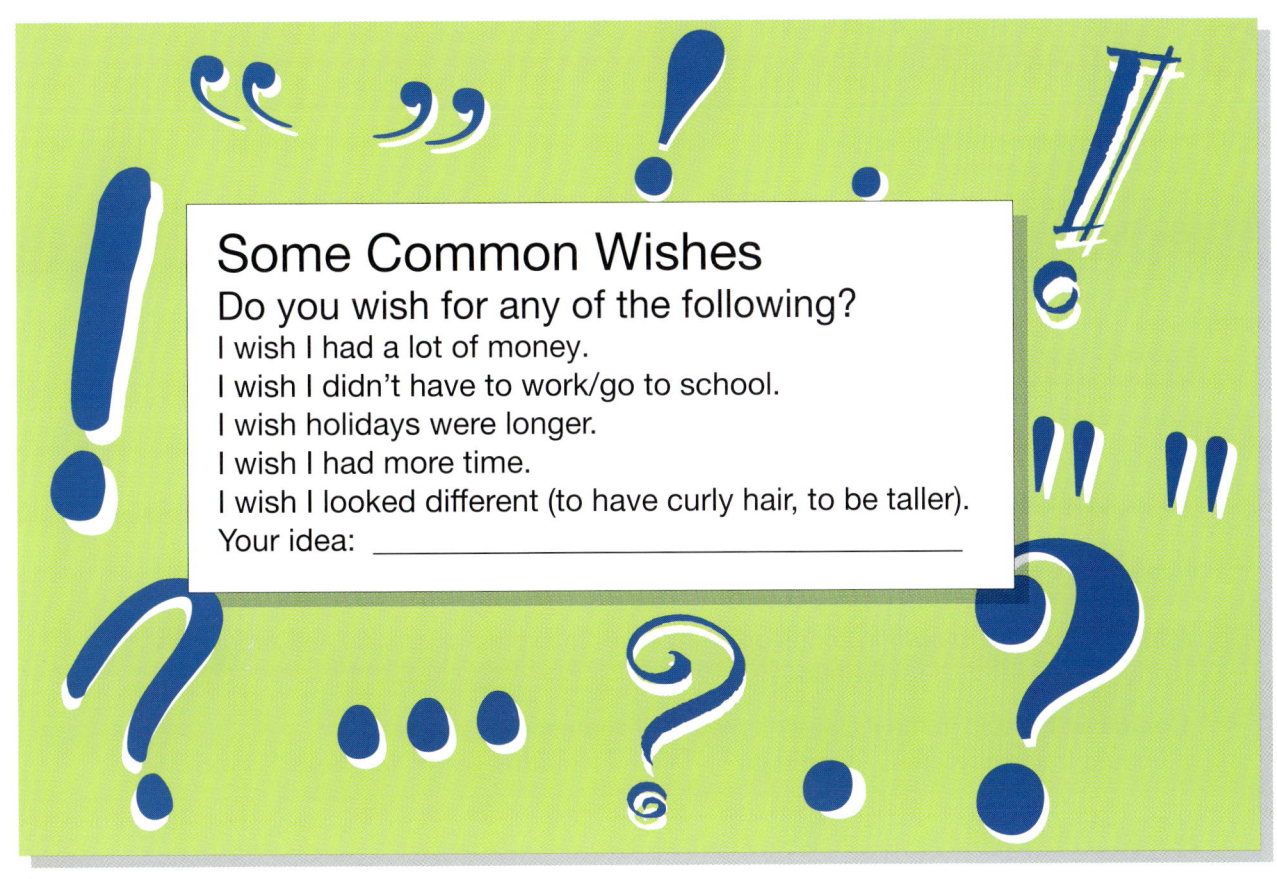

Some Common Wishes

Do you wish for any of the following?
I wish I had a lot of money.
I wish I didn't have to work/go to school.
I wish holidays were longer.
I wish I had more time.
I wish I looked different (to have curly hair, to be taller).
Your idea: _____

1 — COMPREHENSION

Answer *true* or *false*.
1. ____ Angela would take her cell phone to a desert island.
2. ____ Tony would ask an extraterrestrial about life on other planets.
3. ____ Ahmed wouldn't go to the Antarctic.
4. ____ If Mike could live any place in the world, he'd live in Hawaii.
5. ____ If Yoko could be any animal, she would be a whale.
6. ____ Dianne wouldn't like to be Marie Antoinette.

2 — PAIR WORK

A Give your ideas.
You say the *if* clause and your partner completes the rest of the sentence. Use the *if* clauses on these pages. Change roles.

- If I could take only one thing with me to a desert island,
- I'd take my CD player.

B Ask and answer about wishes. You can use the ideas on these pages or your own ideas.

- Do you wish you had a lot of money?
- Yes, I do. Then I would be able to travel.

C Write down your own answers to the questions on page 66 and compare with a partner.

D Write down some common wishes, and compare with your partner.

67

3 GRAMMAR

Second conditional

Use the second conditional to talk about imaginary or hypothetical situations in the present. Use the simple past in the *if* clause.

If I **found** a million dollars, I **would keep** it.   I **wouldn't take** it to the police.

Contractions with *would*

I'd	=	I + would		we'd	=	we + would
you'd	=	you + would		they'd	=	they + would
he'd/she'd	=	he/she + would				

Conditional with *could* and *might*

Might can replace *would* in conditional sentences to express possibility and probability.
If you ask me nicely, I **might take** you with me.

Could can be used in the *if* clause. It means "if someone were able to."
If I **could** travel anywhere, I **would go** to Tahiti. I **wouldn't go** to New York. It's too busy.

Verb *wish*

Use *wish* for things you want to happen but probably won't.

Wish		
in the present	I **don't have** much time.	I **wish** I **had** more time.
	I **have to work** today.	I **wish** I **didn't have to work** today.
	I'm **not** rich.	I **wish** I **was/were** rich.
in the future	He **won't lend** me his car.	I **wish** he **would lend** me his car.

(FYI) *Was* is usually used only in informal spoken English.
I **wish I was/were** a millionaire.

A Match the sentence parts.

1. ___ If I were a very rich person,
2. ___ If I saw someone stealing in a store,
3. ___ If an elevator stopped because of a blackout,
4. ___ If I could say something to the president,
5. ___ If I had to run away from home,
6. ___ If I could choose a profession,

a. I'd tell him/her to cut taxes.
b. I might live with my aunt.
c. I'd be a race car driver.
d. I wouldn't have to work.
e. I'd go to sleep.
f. I'd probably call security.

B Work with a partner. Complete the *if* clauses in **A** with your own ideas.

C Discuss the questions in small groups.
What would you do in the following situations?

1. You found a bag full of money on the street.
2. You saw your best friend's boyfriend/girlfriend with another person.
3. A UFO landed in your neighborhood.
4. You lent a friend some money, but the person didn't return it.
5. You lent a friend a dress or a suit for a special occasion.
   When he/she returned it, it had a big spot on it.

D PROBLEM SOLVING

Work in groups. Pretend your city has the following problems, and you are the government official in charge of solving them. What would you do?

poor public transportation	poor health services
homeless people	poor telephone service
pollution	garbage
crime	few sport facilities
traffic	few libraries
poor schools	expensive housing

E Use the verb **wish** in the following situations. Complete the sentences.
In some cases, more than one verb form can be correct.

> Example:
> Your best friend is a wonderful person, but he/she talks too much.
> I wish that my best friend didn't talk so much/wouldn't talk so much.

1. It's raining again.
   I wish _____.

2. Your father/roommate smokes in the house, and you think it's unhealthy.
   I wish he _____.

3. A friend asked you to a dance, but you don't know how to dance.
   I wish I _____.

4. Your parents won't let you go out tomorrow night.
   I wish they _____.

5. You want to buy someone a present, but you don't have enough money.
   I wish I _____.

6. You have to wear a suit and tie to work.
   I wish we _____.

4 GRAMMAR TALK

- Write one of the following messages, and read it out to the class.
- With the members of your class, select the best messages.

Possibilities:

1. You have to write a message to put into a time capsule for future generations to read. What would you say?

2. You are about to leave your family and friends for a long trip to a remote planet. You don't know if you'll ever come back to Earth. What would you say?

3. You are a castaway on a desert island. You have one bottle to send a message. What would you say?

5 LISTENING

A Listen. Complete the chart with the people's wishes.

	Wish	Why
1. Robin		
Gina		
2. Lynn		
Mark		
3. Oscar		
Sofia		

B Listen again. Try to figure out the reasons for the people's wishes and complete the chart. Share your ideas in small groups.

6 PRONUNCIATION

Listen and practice. Note how **would you** and **could you** are reduced in *Wh-* questions.

/wədʒə/	/kədʒə/
What **would you** do?	What **could you** do?
Where **would you** go?	Where **could you** go?

7 CHAT TIME

1. Do you ever wish you were someone else?
2. What do you wish for at the present time?
3. If your house was on fire, what would be the first thing you'd try to save?
4. If you lived on a desert island, what would you miss most from civilization?
5. Have you ever had a wish come true? Do you know anyone who has?
6. If you could make three wishes, what would you ask for?
7. What advice would you give someone in order to become rich?

8 — CONVERSATION

ALL THE LUCK

Michael: Some people really have all the luck. This guy won a million-dollar jackpot on a game show.

Jennifer: Well, I read about a family that won 100 million dollars in the lottery. Now to me, that would be a real problem. I wouldn't know what to do with so much money.

Michael: You wouldn't know what do with so much money? You have to be crazy. If I won that kind of money, I'd know exactly what to do. I have it all planned out.

Jennifer: What would you do?

Michael: I'd divide the amount into three. One third I'd give to my family, on one condition: that they wouldn't ask me for money ever again. Another third I'd spend on traveling to places I've always dreamed of; I'd buy a house for myself, and a new car, and I'd have a good time.

Jennifer: And what would you do with the rest?

YOUR ENDING
What do you think Michael's answer would be?
① I'd probably give it to charity.
② I'd invest the money in the stock market and try and make more money.
③ I'd give it to you, of course.
④ Your idea: _____

ABOUT THE CONVERSATION
1. Who won money? How did they win it?
2. What would Jennifer do with 100 million dollars?
3. What are two things Michael would do with 100 million dollars?

9 — YOUR TURN

A Role-play the conversation with a partner. Use your endings. Use the answers in About the Conversation as prompts.

B Discuss with a partner what you would do if you won a fortune in the lottery or on a game show.

10 READING

BEFORE READING

1. Have you read the book *Robinson Crusoe* or seen a movie version of it? What was it about? Discuss with a partner.
2. Do you know of books or movies that tell stories of people who are lost in space or are lost in remote areas? Tell about the stories.

> **READING** ⭐
> Use words you know to help you figure out unknown words, such as words that are similar to other English words: for example, *sailor* from *sail*.

Survivor!

What would you do if suddenly you were the sole survivor of a shipwreck or a plane crash and ended up on a desert island? In the 1700s, the English writer Daniel Defoe wrote a famous novel about a shipwrecked sailor named Robinson Crusoe, based on the experiences of a real-life sailor named Alexander Selkirk.

A powerful storm wrecked Crusoe's ship and drowned everyone aboard the ship—except Crusoe. The sea tossed him up on a beach. The ship's wreckage landed near the shore, and Crusoe was able to get a pen and some paper, books, and some tools—all from the ship. After a few days, he climbed a hill and realized that he was on an uninhabited island. Crusoe had to survive by himself!

Crusoe soon discovered that goats lived on the island. He could get milk, butter, cheese, and meat from them. He began to make things for himself: he built a table, a chair, and some shelves. Near the cave with his supplies, he built a well-protected home. Crusoe also began to keep a journal of his experiences. He needed to communicate—if only to himself!

In a small valley, Crusoe found wild grapes and other fruits and vegetables. He dried the grapes to make raisins, which became a favorite food of his. With a few grains of rice and barley from a sack from the ship, the sailor was soon growing large fields of grain. For several years, he experimented with making bread, and he finally succeeded. One of Crusoe's biggest frustrations was the lack of bottles or jars in which he could cook or store food. Over time, he managed to make clay pots that were strong enough to hold liquids.

After four years on the island, he was a different man: "I looked now upon the [civilized] world as a thing remote, which I had nothing to do with, no expectation from, and indeed no desires about."

Crusoe spent his time as a castaway building and inventing. He made a suit from animal skins, as well as an umbrella. He even made a small canoe in which he traveled around the island. He passed twenty-four years in solitude.

Then unexpectedly, while he was walking along the beach one morning, Crusoe saw something frightening—a group of natives with prisoners. The natives were preparing to kill and eat the prisoners. Crusoe managed to drive them off with a gun from the ship. He saved one of the prisoners and named him Friday. His new companion was loyal and intelligent. Friday learned English so that Crusoe had someone to talk to.

Then one day, an English ship anchored near the island. With the help of some crew members, Crusoe gained control of the ship. Although he hated to leave the island, he sailed away on the ship. He had spent twenty-eight years there. Crusoe eventually returned to England to tell his amazing story.

AFTER READING

A Answer the questions.

1. Why was Robinson Crusoe shipwrecked?
2. How did he get milk and cheese on the island?
3. Why was Crusoe able to make bread?
4. What problem did he have in keeping and storing food?
5. Why do you think Robinson named his companion Friday?
6. Was he happy on the island?
   Point out two places in the text where that is mentioned.

B Summarize the story in your own words.

DISCUSSION

1. Have you ever seen any survivor-type programs on television? What are they like? What do you think of them?
2. Why do you think that people are interested in stories of survival in primitive conditions?

11 — WRITING

Write about a movie you saw or a book you read. Write about a story of survival or an adventure story. In the last paragraph, tell about what you would do or how you would feel if you were one of the characters.

> I once read a book called "Girl Against the Jungle." It's about a seventeen-year-old girl who was the only survivor of a plane crash in the jungle of Peru . . .
>
> If I survived a plane crash in the jungle, I would be very scared at first, but then I think I would learn how to . . .

12 — PROJECT

> - Your group is shipwrecked on a desert island. Plan together what you would do to survive.
> - Discuss how you would divide the different tasks among members of the group, based on their individual skills.

9 COMPLAINTS, COMPLAINTS

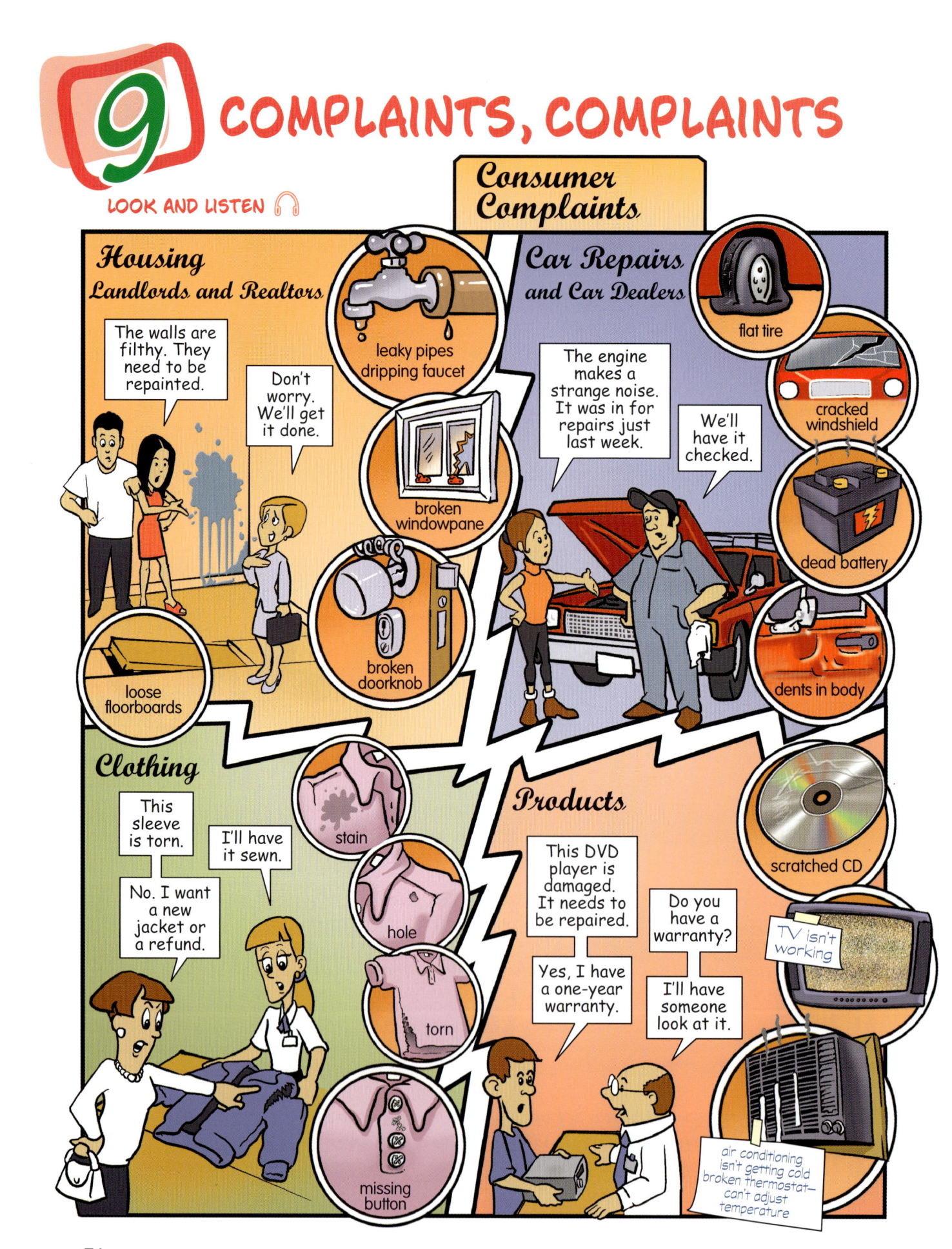

LOOK AND LISTEN 🎧

Consumer Complaints

Housing
Landlords and Realtors

"The walls are filthy. They need to be repainted."

"Don't worry. We'll get it done."

- leaky pipes / dripping faucet
- broken windowpane
- broken doorknob
- loose floorboards

Car Repairs
and Car Dealers

"The engine makes a strange noise. It was in for repairs just last week."

"We'll have it checked."

- flat tire
- cracked windshield
- dead battery
- dents in body

Clothing

"This sleeve is torn."

"I'll have it sewn."

"No. I want a new jacket or a refund."

- stain
- hole
- torn
- missing button

Products

"This DVD player is damaged. It needs to be repaired."

"Do you have a warranty?"

"Yes, I have a one-year warranty."

"I'll have someone look at it."

- scratched CD
- TV isn't working
- air conditioning isn't getting cold / broken thermostat—can't adjust temperature

Consumer Awareness

Know your rights. Are you a wise consumer?
Answer *yes* or *no* to these questions.

	Yes	No

The right to choose
I usually read the information on shelves and the labels on products closely. ☐ ☐
I compare prices of the same brand in different stores. ☐ ☐
I'm not influenced by a pushy salesperson. ☐ ☐

The right to information
I read the advertisements to find out which store offers the best prices. ☐ ☐
I read and compare warranties before purchasing. ☐ ☐

The right to safety
I understand the labels on household products. ☐ ☐
I read the manuals carefully. ☐ ☐

The right to be heard
I usually return products if I'm not satisfied with them. ☐ ☐
I write a letter of complaint if the product or service is not what I expect. ☐ ☐
I always dispute or question an incorrect bill. ☐ ☐

The right to consumer education
I calculate finance charges when I use my credit card(s). ☐ ☐
I don't buy things just because they're on sale. ☐ ☐
I have a good credit record. ☐ ☐
I always request and keep my receipts of purchases. ☐ ☐

1 — COMPREHENSION

A Answer about the complaints.
1. What's wrong with the apartment?
2. What does the woman at the garage say she is going to do?
3. What's wrong with the jacket?
4. What's wrong with the DVD?

Give yourself a point for each *yes*.
11-14: Alert consumer
6-10: You're doing OK.
Below 6: You need improvement.

B Check the good consumer actions.
1. ___ Buy everything in one store because it's more convenient and saves time.
2. ___ Don't let a salesperson push you to buy something.
3. ___ Throw away the manual when you open the box with a new product.
4. ___ Try to determine if you need an item on sale before you buy it.

2 — PAIR WORK

A Do role plays with the problems on page 74.
- What's wrong?
- There's a broken *windowpane*.
- I'll have it *fixed* right away.

B Write down one or two things that show you are a good/bad consumer.
Share them with a partner.

3 GRAMMAR

Need to be done

The windows **need to be cleaned**
The car seats **need to be fixed**.

Have something done

Use **have** or **get** when someone else does the service for you.

The rooms need to be decorated. We're **having/getting** the rooms **decorated**.
The roof needs to be repaired. We're going to **have/get** the roof **repaired**
The house needed to be painted. We **had/got** the house **painted**.

Past participles as adjectives

break–broken The windows were **broken**
crack–cracked The vase was **cracked**.
damage–damaged The disk was **damaged**.
tear–torn The dress was **torn**.

Note: The glass is chipped. It's a **chipped** glass.
The bumper is dented. It's a **dented** bumper.

A Say what is wrong with the following.

Example: The shirt is stained. It needs to be dry-cleaned.

WORD BANK
check, fix, repair, sharpen

B This house has a lot of problems.
  1. Make a list of problems.
  2. Say how you're going to solve them.

Problem	Solution
A windowpane is broken. It needs to be fixed.	I'm going to have it fixed.

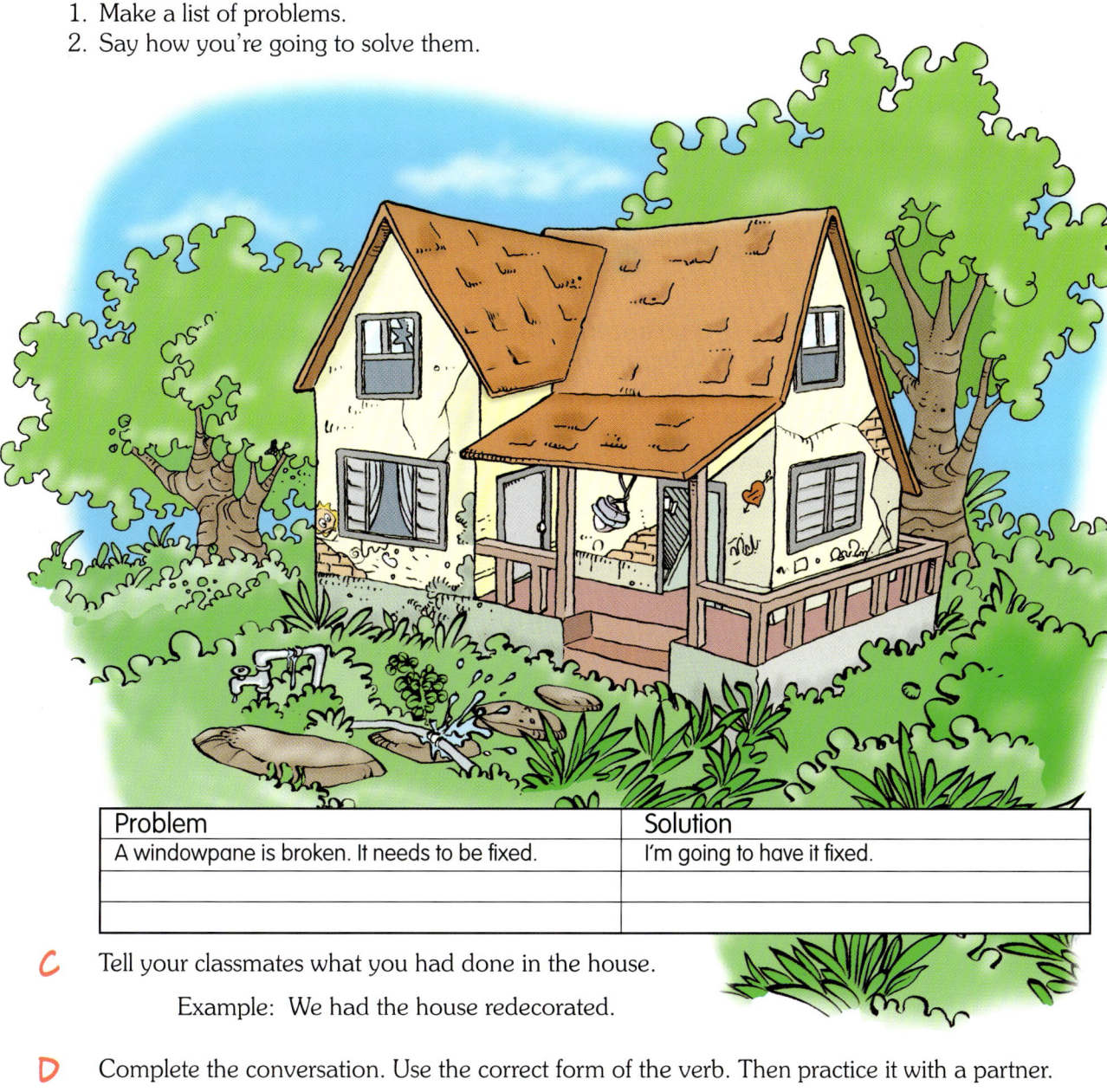

C Tell your classmates what you had done in the house.

   Example: We had the house redecorated.

D Complete the conversation. Use the correct form of the verb. Then practice it with a partner.

Liz: I (have) _____ this car for three months, and it gives me all kinds of problems.
Joe: What is it this time?
Liz: It (not start) _____ in the morning.
Joe: Maybe it's because of the cold, or the battery (might be) _____ dead.
Liz: It isn't that. I (have) _____ a new battery put in, and it still won't start.
      I think the starter needs (repair) _____.
Joe: Is there anything else wrong with the car?
Liz: Yes, the exhaust pipe (fall) _____ off, and the radiator is leaking.
Joe: Is your car under warranty?
Liz: Yes, it is.
Joe: Then you (should not worry) _____. We'll have everything (fix) _____ for you.
Liz: That's what you (say) _____ last time.

77

4 — GRAMMAR TALK

The following silly instructions appeared on product labels.

1. Explain the instructions in your own words. (You might need to correct the English.)
2. Use **should, ought to, must,** or **had better** to give advice.

   Example: You shouldn't use a hairdryer in the bath or in bed.

On a hairdryer
Do not use while sleeping.
Do not use in water.

On a hotel shower cap
Use on one head.

On a dessert
Do not turn container upside down.

On an iron
Do not iron clothes on body.

On a frozen dinner
We suggest you defrost before serving.

On a baby carrier
Put on brakes on slope. It might roll down quickly.

5 — LISTENING

Listen to the guest's complaints. Complete the chart with his problems.

Problem

6 — PRONUNCIATION 🎧

Listen and practice. Each word contains the letter *u*.
Note the different pronunciations.

/uw/	/ʊ/	/ə/
consumer	pushy	product
manual	put	button
dispute		bumper

7 — CHAT TIME

1. Have you ever bought a damaged or defective product?
2. Have you ever returned something to a store? What was the reaction of the person you talked to?
3. Are there organizations that help consumers when they have problems? What do you know about them?
4. What are the most common consumer complaints you know of?

8 — CONVERSATION

THE LATEST FASHION

Salesperson: Can I help you, ma'am?
Margaret: Yes, I'd like to exchange a pair of jeans—baggy with faded colors.
Salesperson: It sounds like one of Kiki's latest creations. She designs loose clothing, and faded clothes are in style this season. You didn't like it?
Margaret: No, it's not that, it's . . .
Salesperson: Of course, ma'am. Can you give me the jeans?
Margaret: You see, they split at the seams, and it happened while I was dancing at a party. I've never felt so embarrassed in my life. Fortunately my friend had a sweater, and I tied it around my waist.
Salesperson: I'm really sorry, ma'am. That's never happened before. Unfortunately the jeans in this department are all made by Kiki.

YOUR ENDING

What do you think was Margaret's response?
① Well, then I want to get the money for the jeans back.
② Can I come back next season when the styles change?
③ Can I get a credit to buy something in another department?
④ Your idea: _____

ABOUT THE CONVERSATION

1. Was the salesperson helpful?
2. What is Kiki's latest style?
3. What was the problem with the jeans?
4. How did Margaret solve the problem at the party?

9 — YOUR TURN

A Role-play the conversation between Margaret and the salesperson.

B Imagine that Margaret has to see the manager about her problem. Write the dialog and present the conversation to the class.

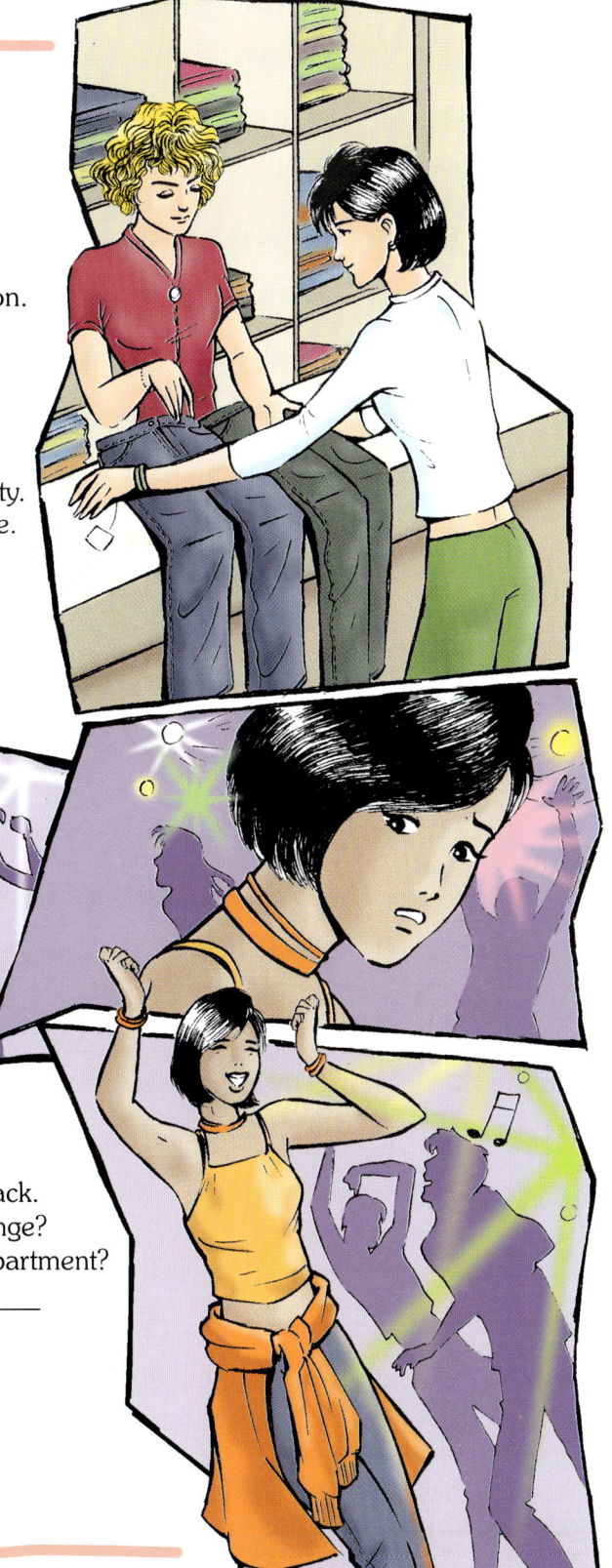

10 — READING

BEFORE READING

Do you believe in bad luck?
Do you think bad luck is just related to chance or coincidence?

> **READING**
> Always try to relate your own experience to examples in a reading.

THE BAD LUCK THEORY

You invite your friends over to watch an NBA basketball playoff game on TV. There are plenty of sodas in the refrigerator, the popcorn is popping, and you are all set to watch the big game. You turn on the set, and all you get is a fuzzy image on the screen. Is this plain bad luck or is it Murphy's law at work? Murphy's law states: "If anything can go wrong, it will."

Similar situations occur all the time. When you're in a hurry to open the door and you try several keys on the key ring, the last one you try is usually the one that works. When you get into a line at the supermarket, you find you've chosen the slowest one, and it just doesn't move. Bad luck or coincidence? According to British physicist Robert Mathews, it's neither one nor the other. He explains that our selective memory tends to remember the bad episodes more readily than the things that usually work out, and the law of probability is more against us than in our favor. For example, in the supermarket with five cashiers, the chances of getting a fast lane are 20 percent, and 80 percent for a slow lane.

Mathews became a popular scientist when he proved that a piece of toast doesn't necessarily fall on the floor on the buttered side. BBC Television gathered 300 people to throw pieces of buttered toast up in the air and observe on which side they fell. Half fell on the buttered side, and half didn't.

Now here's a tricky question for Dr. Mathews. It's a known fact that cats always fall on their four legs. What happens if you tie a piece of buttered toast on a cat's back and drop them from a balcony? Will the cat land on all fours, or will the toast land on the buttered side? I sincerely hope the BBC doesn't try this experiment.

Just remember that you cannot blame Murphy's law for everything that goes wrong. If the hot water runs out while you're having a shower, it's probably because the burner needs to be fixed. If your car breaks down on the way to a job interview, it's probably because you didn't have the vehicle serviced or repaired.

Murphy's Law

Captain Edward Murphy was an engineer at Edwards Air Force Base in the U.S. In 1949, he was working on the project of a machine that measured the heartbeat and breathing of pilots. But something was malfunctioning in the equipment due to human error. Murphy blamed the lab technician and said, "If there is any way to do it wrong, he will." One small failure can bring a whole project crashing down. In practice, it was a good principle of safety engineering, and it became popular in all areas to explain the failures of everyday things.

AFTER READING
1. What does the example of the NBA game illustrate?
2. What does Murphy's law state?
3. According to Robert Mathews, how does the law of probability work against us in the supermarket line?
4. Why did Mathews do the buttered bread experiment? What did it show?

DISCUSSION
Do you believe in Murphy's Law?

11 — WRITING

Write a letter of complaint about a faulty product.

> Dear Sir/Madam:
>
> I'm writing to complain about the *Multi-Lingua* electronic translator which I bought from Gadgets Store recently and which is still under warranty. The instructions said the machine could translate into ten different languages; however, when I ask for Spanish, I get Chinese, and when . . .

12 — PROJECT

- Imagine you work for a consumer protection organization in your country.
- Identify the most frequent complaints. Choose one complaint and write advice to consumers.
- Present to the class.

EXPANSION 3

1 — READING

BEFORE READING

What do you know about the origin of soccer, basketball, and baseball? Discuss with a partner.

POPULAR SPORTS

SOCCER

Soccer has been played for thousands of years throughout history by various civilizations. In 2500 B.C., the Chinese played a form of the game and called it *Tsu Chu*. One story tells of a brave village in England defeating a Roman team and running them out of town in 217 A.D. The natives of the Pacific Islands played the game using their hands and feet, and they used coconuts and pig bladders as balls. The Eskimos played soccer on ice and used balls filled with caribou hair and grass. In North America, Indians played on beaches with fields that had enough space for 1,000 players to be playing at the same time, and the match usually lasted for more than one day. The games were so rough that the players often got broken bones. In Mexico and Central America, they invented the rubber ball, and the people played in courts 40-50 feet (12-15 meters) long surrounded by vertical walls several feet high. In the middle of each wall there was a stone with a hole in the middle or a wooden ring, and the idea was for players to project the hard rubber ball through the ring. But it was not until 1863 in England that the first set of rules was put together to make the game like it is today. Soccer was spread throughout the world by British sailors and settlers, and all major innovations in the game such as leagues, professionalism, and international matches were English.

BASKETBALL

In 1891, Dr. James A. Naismith, a teacher at the YMCA school in Springfield, Massachusetts, in the U.S., was asked to create a game that could be played indoors during the hard winters. Students were tired of staying inside, and they looked forward to any sporting activity. So Naismith put up two peach baskets on opposite walls and got his class of eighteen students to play a game of "basketball." The team that dropped the ball into the basket more times would win. At first a soccer ball was used, but in 1894, it was decided that the ball should be 81 centimeters around and weigh 500 grams. In spite of all the changes that have taken place since then, the size of the ball has remained the same, but the weight increased to 600 grams. The baskets used in early games had the bottoms in them, and after each goal someone had to climb a ladder in order to get the ball out. In 1906, open baskets were introduced, which allowed the ball to pass through, and as a result the game became faster. In the beginning, no backboards were used either. Therefore, fans sitting in the balcony behind the basket would push away the ball when the opponent was going to score. Also in the early days, each team was made up of nine players. It wasn't until 1897 that the five-player team became official.

BASEBALL

Baseball originated from cricket and an old English game called *rounders*. Children in Boston during Colonial times used to play it using four bases and a batter's box. One legend said that Abner Doubleday was the person who, in 1839 in Cooperstown, New York, developed the game played on the diamond-shaped field with four bases and named the game *baseball*. Although Doubleday had been given credit for his invention, baseball historians say it was Alexander Cartwright and his friends that devised the new game in 1845. It was called *the Knickerbocker game* or *the New York game,* and it differed in several respects from what we now know as baseball. For instance, they caught the ball barehanded, but fortunately the ball was a lot lighter than the one used today; it was slightly larger and very bouncy, because it contained a core of Indian rubber. There was no umpire saying whether a pitch was a ball or a strike. The batter could just stand at home plate and wait, all day if he had to, until he got a pitch he wanted to swing at. Also, while today a ball has to be caught before it hits the ground in order to be considered an out, a ball caught on the first bounce was considered an out in the Knickerbocker game.

AFTER READING

A Answer *true* or *false* about the texts.

1. _____ Although soccer had been played for hundreds of years, the first set of rules was only established in 1863.
2. _____ If the Indians had played on regular fields, there wouldn't have been enough space for all the players.
3. _____ In Central America, the idea was for players to hit the ring with the ball.
4. _____ Before basketball, people weren't used to playing games indoors during the hard winters in the U.S.
5. _____ In the early days of basketball, the game ended as soon as one of the players managed to drop the ball into one of the baskets.
6. _____ If a batter hit the ball during a Knickerbocker game and it was caught after the first bounce, he would be out.

B Read the texts again and list the words related to games in the following categories.

GAME	VERBS	NOUNS	ADJECTIVES
SOCCER	play	player	rough
BASKETBALL			
BASEBALL			

C Describe the origin of one of the games in your own words.

2 ACTIVITIES

Complete the interview with a sports star.
Use the correct form of each word in parentheses.

A: You've just been sold to *Real Madrid* for $100 million. I was wondering how much of that money actually goes into your pocket.
B: I wish it (be) _____ that amount. In fact, it was half of that. I get only ten percent if I'm lucky, my agent and the club get the rest.
A: How much do you get from (play) _____?
B: About six million a year.
A: Plus all the money you make from advertising. Some people think you soccer players are overpaid.
B: I disagree. We might (make) _____ a lot of money, but our careers are very short. By the time we (be) _____ thirty, we're burned out. We have (crack) _____ heads, (tear) _____ ligaments, and (break) _____ ribs. Very few players continue after that.
A: If you could, would you?
B: No, I wouldn't. I'm thinking of (retire) _____ at twenty-eight.
A: And are you looking forward to (play) _____ in Spain?
B: Yes, I'm used to (play) _____ in different clubs and living in different places.

3 — WRITING

Choose one of the following to write about and give your opinion.

1. Nowadays sports like soccer, basketball, and baseball are big business and generate billions of dollars all over the world. Sometimes players can earn more from advertising than they can playing the game.
2. Sports celebrities are also looked upon as role models. Some players live up to the image they have formed, but others are bad examples to be followed.
3. The passion for sports can sometimes result in violence. The worst soccer riot in history began when a goal was annulled by the referee during a qualifying match between Argentina and Peru in 1964; 309 people were killed and 1,000 were injured in Lima. A World Cup qualifying match between Honduras and El Salvador led to the "Soccer War" between those two nations in 1969. Nowadays instead of enjoying the game and rooting for their team, many spectators resort to violence and hooliganism.

4 — TALK ABOUT IT

1. What is your favorite sport? Describe how it is played.
2. Are you a fan of any particular team? What do you do when your team wins?
3. Who is the most popular sports star in your country?
4. What advantages and disadvantages do sports stars have?
5. What would you do if you were a famous sports star and earned a lot of money? How would you behave?
6. What is the general opinion in your country about the three topics in the Writing?

10 I WONDER WHAT HAPPENED

LOOK AND LISTEN 🎧

- Whoever threw that rock must have been really strong.
- It can't have been a person. Who would do something like that?
- Whatever it is, it certainly made a big hole in her car!
- It might have fallen off a truck.
- It can't be a rock. It's too heavy. It must be a cannonball.
- Whenever you leave your car parked on the street, anything could happen.
- It's the same thing wherever you go.

IT'S RAINING ROCKS!

Cheryl Watkins had parked her car and had gone shopping. When she returned, she found that a rock had fallen on her brand new car. The impact was so great that it had gone through the roof, and had landed on the driver's seat. The wheels of the car had also been bent. And how big was the rock? About the size of a melon. What could have happened? Who would throw a rock this size, and with such force? Someone said that a man was seen looking down from the top of a nearby building. It must have been him. The police were called immediately, and the object was taken to police headquarters.

But when detective Meyers saw the black rock and felt its weight, he started laughing. He knew exactly what it was. He had seen many of those when he had been in the desert in the army. It was a meteorite. It could have landed anywhere, but it chose to hit Cheryl's car. One other problem: Cheryl's car insurance doesn't cover damage from meteorites.

1 — COMPREHENSION

Answer *true* or *false*.
1. ____ Cheryl had left her car parked in the street.
2. ____ Someone must have thrown the rock from a building.
3. ____ It might have been a cannonball.
4. ____ No one could have thrown a rock with that force.
5. ____ The detective had never seen a rock like that before.
6. ____ When Cheryl got back to her car, the vehicle had been crushed.

2 — PAIR WORK

A   Ask and answer about the picture.

- What might have happened?
- The rock might have fallen off a passing truck.

- What do you think it is?
- It can't be a satellite. It must be a meteorite.

B   Write down what you think *might*, *could*, or *must* have happened and compare with a partner.

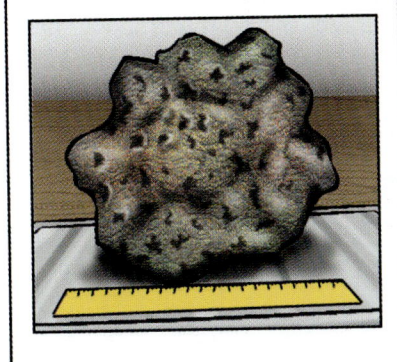

3 — GRAMMAR

Past perfect tense

Use **the past perfect tense** (*had* + past participle) to indicate which action happened before another in the past.

When we **arrived** in the airport, our flight **had** already **left**.
They **couldn't get** in the house, because they **had forgotten** the key.

Question (+)	Short answer (+)	Short answer (-)
Had I/you/he/she/we/they been there before?	Yes, I/you/he/she/we/they had.	No, I/you/he/she/we/they hadn't.

Can't be/might be/must be

Use *can't be*, *might be* or *must be* to make suppositions, to speculate about something, and to draw conclusions.

Present

It **can't be** a balloon. Balloons aren't shaped like that. It **might be** a glider. But gliders don't fly vertically. It **must be** a helicopter.

Past

It **can't have been** a balloon. Balloons aren't shaped like that. It **might have been** a glider. But gliders don't fly vertically. It **must have been** a helicopter.

Whatever, whoever, whenever, wherever

Whatever = anything (that) / everything (that)
Whoever = anyone (who) / everyone (who)
Whenever = any time / every time
Wherever = anywhere / everywhere

You must do **whatever** she says.
Whoever finishes first wins.
I visit Grandma **whenever** I can.
Wherever he is, he must be happy.

A Use the simple past and the past perfect to complete the sentences.

1. I (feel) _____ much better after I (see) _____ the results of my test.
2. It was raining, but by the time we (arrive) _____, the rain (stop) _____.
3. Dinosaurs (be) _____ extinct for millions of years before the first humans (appear) _____.
4. I (never, travel) _____ outside my country until I (go) _____ to Disney World.
5. We wanted to get a picture of the meteorite, but when we (arrive), _____ the police (already, take) _____ it away.
6. No, Your Honor, I (not see) _____ that man before the night he (break into) _____ my apartment.

B Use *whatever*, *wherever*, *whenever*, or *whoever*.

1. Raymond is a very friendly person. He makes friends _____ he goes.
2. _____ solved that problem was extremely smart.
3. I'll do _____ I have to do so that we can finish the work on time.
4. I always make a wish _____ I see a falling star.
5. When I was a kid, I ate _____ my Mom gave me.
6. "To our listeners in Europe, Asia, or _____ you are, this is Carol Mathews, saying good night!"

C Look at the pictures, and explain what you think.
Use *must have happened*, *might have happened*, and *could have happened*.

Example:
He must have walked in the rain.
It might have been raining.
Someone could have dropped a bucket of water on him.

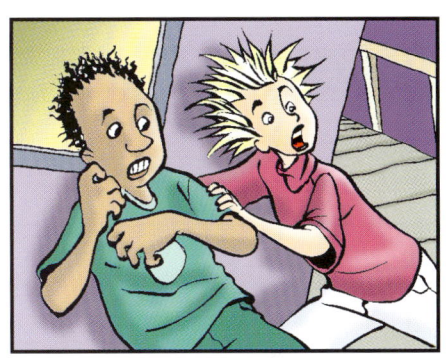

89

4 — GRAMMAR TALK

Look at the pictures and guess what they **might be**, **can't be**, or **must be**.

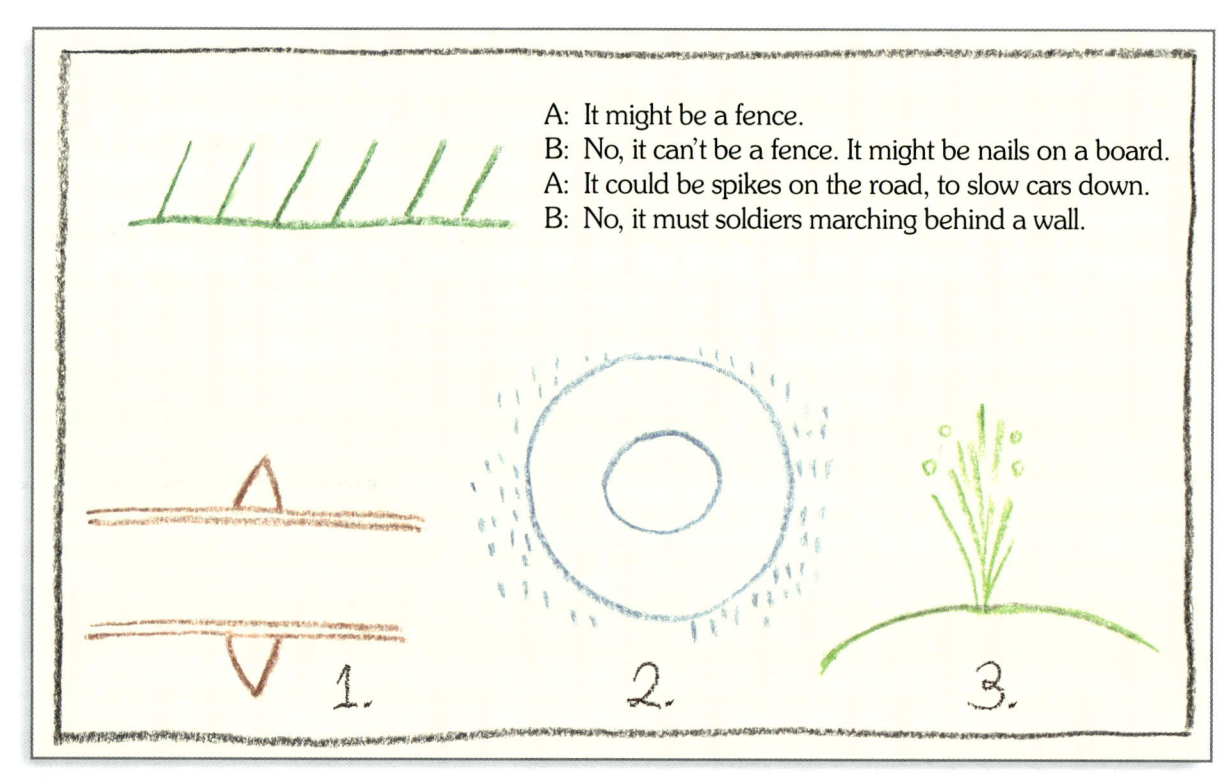

A: It might be a fence.
B: No, it can't be a fence. It might be nails on a board.
A: It could be spikes on the road, to slow cars down.
B: No, it must soldiers marching behind a wall.

1.   2.   3.

Possible answers:
1. a canoe under a bridge 2. a flying saucer; someone wearing a sombrero 3. a burst pipe; a whale blowing out water; a geyser

5 — LISTENING

Listen to the two strange events and complete the chart.

	What happened?	Speculation/Possibility
Cochabamba, Bolivia		
Fred and Mildred's ranch		

6 — PRONUNCIATION 🎧

Listen and practice.
Note the *-er* ending in the following words.

/ər/

Whatever you do is better than nothing.
I eat butter whenever I can.
Whoever wrote this is very clever.
I write a letter from wherever I travel.

7 — CHAT TIME

1. Have you ever seen a meteorite?
2. Have you ever left your car parked somewhere, and when you came back something had happened to it?
3. Have you ever heard or read about unusual incidents that were hard to explain?
4. Have you ever seen a candid camera-type program? Tell about it.

8 — CONVERSATION

Steve: I wonder what they're doing behind that wall.
Emily: They must be putting up a new high-rise. All the old buildings in this area are being demolished to make room for these horrible skyscrapers.
Steve: It can't be. There isn't any noise coming from there.
Emily: They might have already finished digging the foundations.
Steve: Well, if they had done that, there would still be cranes and machinery around.
Emily: It could be a new parking lot. If I owned space in the center of town, that's what I would do.
Steve: Let's check it out.
Emily: OK.

* * *

Steve: There's a hole in the wall.
Emily: And there's a sign that says "Don't look!"
Steve: Well, this is a free country, and I'm going to have a look. Hey! What are you doing?
Emily: Steve, your face is all full of paint. Ha! Ha! Ha!
Woman: Look over there! You're on "Candid Camera."

ABOUT THE CONVERSATION
1. What does Emily think they must be doing behind the wall?
2. Why does Steve disagree?
3. What would there be on the site if they were building?
4. What does Emily think it could be?
5. Explain in your own words what happened to Steve.

9 — YOUR TURN

A Role-play the conversation with a partner. Speculate about what is behind the scaffolding.

B Continue the dialog between the woman and Steve.

C Prepare a "candid camera" situation with a partner and present it to the class.

10 — READING

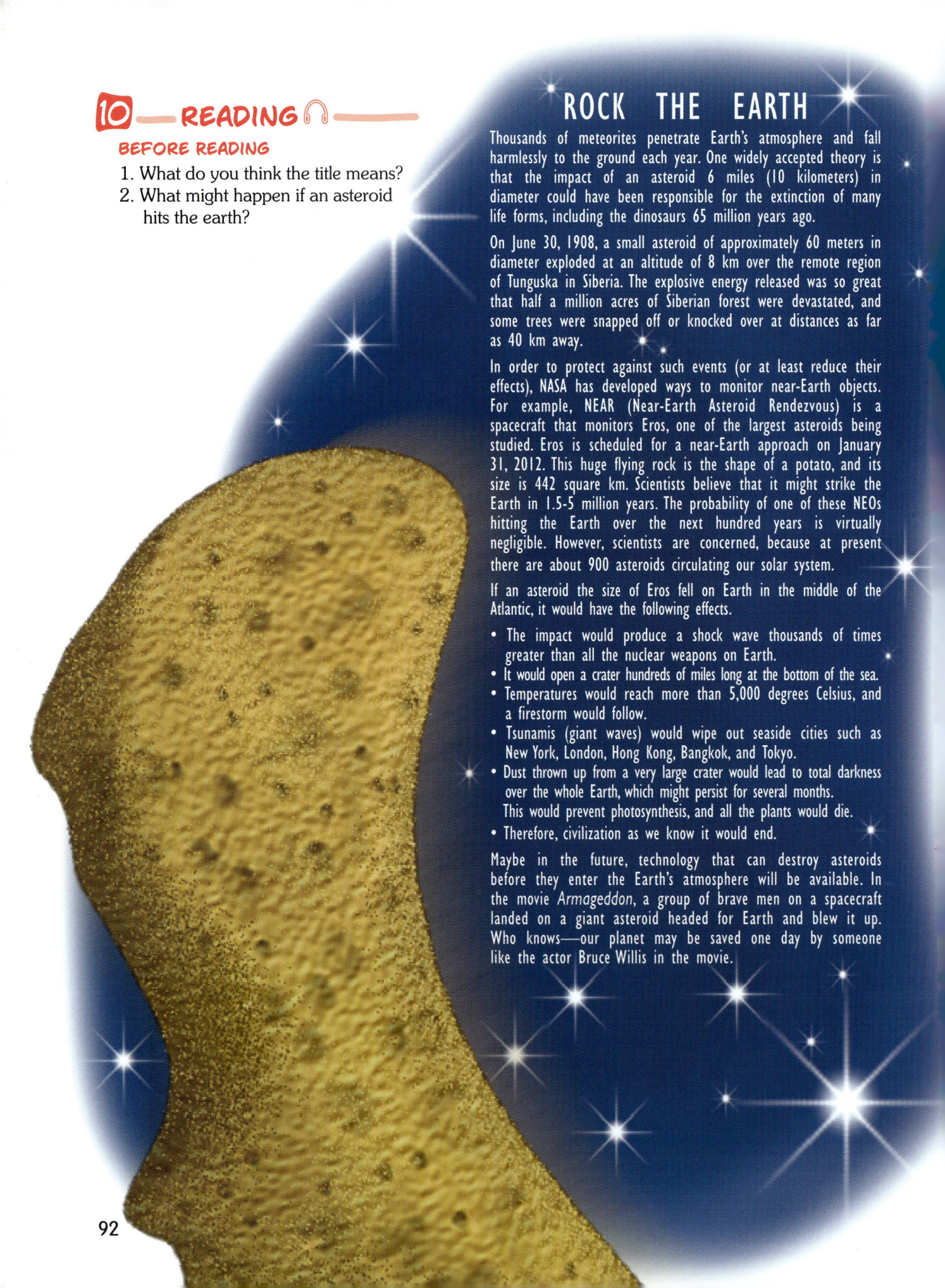

BEFORE READING

1. What do you think the title means?
2. What might happen if an asteroid hits the earth?

ROCK THE EARTH

Thousands of meteorites penetrate Earth's atmosphere and fall harmlessly to the ground each year. One widely accepted theory is that the impact of an asteroid 6 miles (10 kilometers) in diameter could have been responsible for the extinction of many life forms, including the dinosaurs 65 million years ago.

On June 30, 1908, a small asteroid of approximately 60 meters in diameter exploded at an altitude of 8 km over the remote region of Tunguska in Siberia. The explosive energy released was so great that half a million acres of Siberian forest were devastated, and some trees were snapped off or knocked over at distances as far as 40 km away.

In order to protect against such events (or at least reduce their effects), NASA has developed ways to monitor near-Earth objects. For example, NEAR (Near-Earth Asteroid Rendezvous) is a spacecraft that monitors Eros, one of the largest asteroids being studied. Eros is scheduled for a near-Earth approach on January 31, 2012. This huge flying rock is the shape of a potato, and its size is 442 square km. Scientists believe that it might strike the Earth in 1.5-5 million years. The probability of one of these NEOs hitting the Earth over the next hundred years is virtually negligible. However, scientists are concerned, because at present there are about 900 asteroids circulating our solar system.

If an asteroid the size of Eros fell on Earth in the middle of the Atlantic, it would have the following effects.

- The impact would produce a shock wave thousands of times greater than all the nuclear weapons on Earth.
- It would open a crater hundreds of miles long at the bottom of the sea.
- Temperatures would reach more than 5,000 degrees Celsius, and a firestorm would follow.
- Tsunamis (giant waves) would wipe out seaside cities such as New York, London, Hong Kong, Bangkok, and Tokyo.
- Dust thrown up from a very large crater would lead to total darkness over the whole Earth, which might persist for several months. This would prevent photosynthesis, and all the plants would die.
- Therefore, civilization as we know it would end.

Maybe in the future, technology that can destroy asteroids before they enter the Earth's atmosphere will be available. In the movie *Armageddon*, a group of brave men on a spacecraft landed on a giant asteroid headed for Earth and blew it up. Who knows—our planet may be saved one day by someone like the actor Bruce Willis in the movie.

AFTER READING

A Answer the questions.

1. What could have caused the extinction of dinosaurs?
2. What was the result of the explosion of the meteorite over Siberia?
3. What is the purpose of the NEAR project?
4. What do scientists believe might happen in 1.5 million years?
5. Which sentence in the text summarizes what would happen if a giant meteor hit the earth?

B Find words in the text that mean:

1. distant _____
2. worried _____
3. crash into _____
4. destroy _____
5. hole _____

DISCUSSION

What would you do if you discovered that a big asteroid was going to hit the earth in about a month? Write down what you would or might do and compare your list with a partner.

11 — WRITING

Write about an unusual occurrence or a discovery that impressed you.

Thor Heyerdahl, the Swedish explorer, believed that Easter Island and the rest of the Pacific had been inhabited by people who had come originally from South America. So in 1947, he decided to prove that pre-Inca people could have sailed to the islands in the Pacific. Thor and four companions set sail from Peru on a raft identical to those used by the Incas. After 101 days, the *Kon-Tiki* arrived in Rangiroa, French Polynesia, 4,300 miles away.

12 — PROJECT

- *In a group, look up incidents that have occurred on Earth involving meteorites.*
- *Choose one and present your findings to the class.*

11 IF I'D ONLY KNOWN

LOOK AND LISTEN

LOOKING BACK
Life's Regrets

At one time or another we all look back and wish we had done things differently in our lives. The following are some typical situations.

Things you should/shouldn't have done

IF ONLY I'D LISTENED TO MY MOTHER, I WOULDN'T BE CARRYING THESE BOXES.

He should have studied harder at school. If he had listened to his mother, he would have gone to college.

I SHOULD HAVE MARRIED MY HIGH SCHOOL SWEETHEART.

If she had known they were going to argue and fight, she wouldn't have married him.

Things you should/shouldn't have said

GRANDPA, YOU SHOULDN'T HAVE BOUGHT THAT.

She should have told her grandfather that she loved him. He would have been really happy.

YOU SHOULD HAVE FINISHED THE JOB. YOU'RE SO SLOW!

He should have told his boss that he shouldn't treat his employees like that.

How about you?

A Mark what you would have said or done in the situations on page 94.

1. a. ___ I would have listened to my Mom, and I would have gone to college.
   b. ___ I wouldn't have listened, and I would have gone my own way.

2. a. ___ I would have married him/her if we loved each other.
   b. ___ If we argued about things, I wouldn't have married him/her.

3. a. ___ I would have told him that I loved him more often.
   b. ___ I wouldn't have said anything, because he knew I loved him.

4. a. ___ I would have told him not to treat me like that.
   b. ___ I wouldn't have said anything, and I would have left the job.

B Write another possibility for each situation on page 94.

1. _____
2. _____
3. _____
4. _____

1 — COMPREHENSION

Answer *true* or *false*.

1. ___ The man regrets that he didn't listen to his mother.
2. ___ The girl doesn't want to accept the present.
3. ___ The woman is sorry she married her husband.
4. ___ The man's boss thinks he's taking too long to finish.

2 — PAIR WORK

A Ask and answer.

- What should I have <u>studied</u>?
- You should have <u>studied engineering</u>.

- If I had known you were coming, I would have <u>cooked your favorite meal</u>.
- That's OK, Mom. You shouldn't worry about that.

- What would you have done if you'd been me?
- I would have done it my way.

B If you could look back, what mistakes would you try to avoid? Write down a list and compare with a partner.

3 GRAMMAR

Should have + past participle

Use **should** + **past participle** to talk about regrets.

I **should have said** I was sorry. I **shouldn't have done** that.

The third conditional

Use **if** + **past perfect** with **would** + **present perfect** to talk about things that didn't happen in the past, to talk about things you would have done differently, or for advice.

If I **had studied** a little harder, I **would have passed** the exam.
If I **had known** before, I **wouldn't have lent** him the money.
If I **had been** you, I **would have told** him to stop the car immediately.

FYI — I'd = I + had or I + would

If with could and might

Use **if** + **past perfect** with **could/might** + **present perfect** to talk about possibilities and missed opportunities.

If I **had gotten** a job last summer, I **could have saved** more money.
If she **had left** work earlier, she **might have avoided** traffic.

A Read the situations and make sentences using **should have/shouldn't have**.

1. I lent April some money, but she never paid me back.
2. Bob forgot his key, so he broke the window to get into the house.
3. Mary didn't feel well, but she didn't want to go to the doctor.
4. Jerry was upset because we didn't ask him to go out with us.
5. We went to Gino's Restaurant, but the food wasn't good.
6. Mr. Johnson missed a really important meeting last night.

B Now complete these sentences about people in A.

If I had been April, I would have _____.
If I had been Bob, I could have _____.
If I had been Mary, I might have _____.

C Make sentences.

1. ___ If I had known it was going to rain,
2. ___ If she had asked me for advice,
3. ___ If I had had enough money,
4. ___ If you had been home,
5. ___ If they had told the truth,
6. ___ If I hadn't moved out of the way,
7. ___ If the referee hadn't helped them,

a. I would have told her not to marry him.
b. they wouldn't have gotten into trouble.
c. their team wouldn't have won the game.
d. I would have been run over.
e. I would have taken an umbrella.
f. I would have visited you.
g. I would have bought a plane ticket.

D Now use the first part of the sentences in Activity C and add your own endings.

E Work with a partner.
What **should**, **would**, **could**, or **might** you have said or done in the following situations? Compare with other pairs.

1. It was late at night when Ken remembered he hadn't taken the garbage out. He was already in his pajamas, but he wasn't going to get dressed again just for that. So he went outside quickly, threw the bags into the trash can, and rushed back to the house. When he got to the front door he realized he had locked himself out. He was busy trying to break into the house when a police officer saw him.
2. You saw an old friend at the airport that you hadn't seen in years. You went up to him or her, greeted the person, and started talking about old times. Suddenly you realize that you had made a mistake.
3. Gloria borrowed her boyfriend's car and dented it. She returned it, but she didn't say anything about it. The following day, when they went out, her boyfriend noticed the dent and thought that someone in the parking lot had bumped into his car.
4. It was a special occasion, and you wanted to celebrate. You invited a friend to go out to a fancy restaurant. The meal was wonderful, and you enjoyed the evening. When the waiter brought the bill, you realized you had forgotten your wallet at home.

4 — GRAMMAR TALK

The following message was found in a bottle. Imagine you found it. Discuss with a partner what you would have thought if you had found the bottle and what you would have done with the money.

In 1949, Jack Wurm, an unemployed man, was aimlessly walking on a California beach when he came across a bottle that had floated to the beach containing this message: "To avoid confusion, I leave my entire estate to the lucky person who finds this bottle and to my attorney, Barry Cohen, share and share alike. Daisy Alexander, June 20, 1937." It was not a hoax. Mr. Wurm received over $6 million from the Alexander estate.

5 — LISTENING

Listen to the people on the radio show and complete the chart.

Name	Regret	Reason
Sheila		
Fred		

6 — PRONUNCIATION

Listen and practice.
Notice the reduction of **could have**, **should have**, and **would have**.

> I **could have** traveled.
> He **should have** studied harder.
> He **would have** been really happy.

7 — CHAT TIME

1. What mistakes have you made in your life?
2. What things do you regret not having done in your life?
3. What things would you have done differently?
4. Talk about the best or worse thing that has ever happened to you.
5. Have you ever been in an embarrassing situation or a predicament? Tell about it.

8 CONVERSATION

Raphael: So what did you do when you graduated?
Cecilia: I got my master's degree, and then I got a really good job. There were 100 candidates, but I got the position.
Raphael: Congratulations!
Cecilia: Yeah. But I wish I had done things differently. I think I was too immature.
Raphael: But now you have a stable job, and a career.
Cecilia: And all the responsibility. I should have listened to my parents. I could have traveled, I could have done all kinds of things, but I had my mind set on my career. What about you?
Raphael: I went to study in London. If it hadn't been for my parents, I wouldn't have gone.
Cecilia: What was it like there?
Raphael: I shared a "flat" with three girls. I waited on tables, and even catered to royalty at the Royal Albert Hall. When I finished my courses, I bought a second-hand car with the money I'd saved, and I drove all the way across Europe with a friend as far as Turkey. We were on the road for six months.
Cecilia: That must have been a great experience.
Raphael: It certainly was. Now I have to get a job and think about my financial situation. But if I could, I'd do it all over again.

ABOUT THE CONVERSATION
1. What did Cecilia do after she graduated?
2. What would Cecilia have done differently?
3. Who encouraged Raphael to go to London?
4. What did he do there?
5. Does Raphael regret what he did?
6. What would you have done if you had been Cecilia or Raphael?

9 YOUR TURN

A Role-play the conversation.

B Pretend you are talking to Raphael or Cecilia. Talk about the things you would have done differently.

10 READING

BEFORE READING

1. Do you ever read advice columns in newspapers and magazines?
2. What kind of help do they give?

• Lillian and Jeff • Lillian and Jeff • Lillian and Jeff • Lillian and Jeff • Lillian and Jeff • Lillian and Jeff • Lillian and Jeff •

Lillian and Jeff

ADVICE COLUMN

Dear Lillian and Jeff:

I am writing to tell you a story. It's too late for you to tell me what to do now, but maybe you could tell me what I should have done. Your advice might be useful to others in similar situations.

My best friend, Sue, has been dating a guy for six months. She really likes him. I always had my doubts about her boyfriend. We sometimes went out on dates together, and he always seemed to notice other women.

Well, a week ago, I went out dancing with a few friends to a club in a different part of town. I saw Sue's boyfriend there with another woman. They were dancing and having fun together, and they didn't notice me. Someone at the club said that they were often there together.

I didn't know what to do, but I decided to tell my friend. Well, she asked her boyfriend, and he said it was a one-time night out, and that I wanted to make trouble. Now Sue is mad at me.

Now I wish that I hadn't said anything to Sue. What do you think I should have done? Should I have just not said anything? Would that have been fair to Sue?

Confused in L.A.

• Lillian and Jeff • Lillian and Jeff • Lillian and Jeff • Lillian and Jeff • Lillian and Jeff • Lillian and Jeff • Lillian and Jeff •

100

• Lillian and Jeff • Lillian and Jeff • Lillian and Jeff • Lillian and Jeff • Lillian and Jeff • Lillian and Jeff • Lillian and Jeff •

Dear Lillian and Jeff:

I'm a taxi driver, and people leave all kinds of things in my cab—scarves, shoes, packages. But last week someone left a briefcase full of money! I didn't count it, but there must have been at least $100,000.

It was a businessman who left the case. His destination was the most elegant hotel in the city. His name was on the case, so I called the hotel and asked for him. He was grateful, and he said that he was going to give me a reward. Well, when I got there, he gave me $50. I was very disappointed, and thought to myself that I should just have kept the money.

Since then, I've been thinking of all the things that I could have done with the money. I could have bought myself a new cab—or at least put a down payment on one. I could have taken my family on a vacation. I could have sent my children to a private school.

Did I do the right thing?

Honest, but wondering why

AFTER READING
1. What happened in the club?
2. What does the person wish he or she hadn't done?
3. What did the cab driver find?
4. What does the cab driver think he or she shouldn't have done?
5. What does the cab driver think he or she could have done?

DISCUSSION
1. What should Sue have done?
2. What should the passenger have done?
3. Discuss a problem you or a friend is having, and ask for advice.

Lillian and Jeff

• Lillian and Jeff • Lillian and Jeff • Lillian and Jeff • Lillian and Jeff • Lillian and Jeff • Lillian and Jeff • Lillian and Jeff •

11 — WRITING

Imagine you are Lillian or Jeff.
Write an answer to Sue or the passenger, telling him or her what you think he or she should have done.

Dear X or Y:

You shouldn't have done what you did. If I had been you, I would have ...

12 — PROJECT

- Imagine that you could be born again.
  In a group, list the things that you would have done/wouldn't have done.
- Compare your lists with the other groups in the class.

12 WHAT THEY SAID

LOOK AND LISTEN

"And now we would like to bring you our "QUOTES OF THE WEEK.""

"Professor, do you believe that intelligent life exists elsewhere in the universe?"

"No, I don't. The positive proof is that no one has bothered to make contact with us."

Professor Marvin said that the proof that intelligent life didn't exist is that no one had bothered to make contact with us.

"I will build bridges, even in places where there are no rivers."

The presidential candidate said he would build bridges even in places where there were no rivers.

1 — COMPREHENSION

Answer *true* or *false*.

1. ____ The professor said there was no life elsewhere because no one had bothered to contact us.
2. ____ The candidate said that he wouldn't build bridges everywhere.
3. ____ The teacher asked Johnny if he knew what the inhabits of Moscow were called.
4. ____ Janine told reporters that the doctors hadn't found anything wrong with her.

2 — PAIR WORK

A Ask and answer about the quotes.

- What did the reporter ask the professor?
- She asked him if there was intelligent life elsewhere in the universe.

- What did Janine Hollyfield say about her head?
- She said that the doctors had taken an X-ray and had found nothing.

B Write down other things the people might have said, and have your partner relate your statements.

3 — GRAMMAR

Reported Speech

Direct speech	Reported speech

Simple present
"I **have** a brother and a sister."
"I **don't like** mangoes."

Simple past
He said he **had** a brother and a sister.
She said she **didn't like** mangoes.

Present progressive
"I**'m talking** to Mary."

Past progressive
She said she **was talking** to Mary.

Simple past
"I **learned** English in Canada."

Past perfect
He said he **had learned** English in Canada.

Present perfect
"I **haven't seen** the movie yet."

Past perfect
She said she **hadn't seen** the movie yet.

Modals
"I**'ll see** you later."
"I **can't come** to the meeting."
"I **have to/must go** to the doctor."

She said she **would see** me later.
He said he **couldn't come** to the meeting.
She said she **had to/must go** to the doctor.

Reported questions
How old **are** you?
Where **were** you last night?

He asked how old I **was**.
She wanted to know where I **had been** the night before.

Note: If there is no question word (*how*, *where*, *when*, etc.), **if** is used.

Are you a student?
Did you **enjoy** the party?

He asked **if I was** a student.
She asked **if I had enjoyed** the party.

Word changes
Sometimes, in reported speech, the words may be different from those in the original sentence.

"Why aren't you at school?"
"Of course I did my homework."
"You should leave now."
"I think it's a good idea."

Mother **asked/wanted to know** why she wasn't at school.
Tom **assured** the teacher that he had done his homework.
Mary **suggested** we should leave **right away**.
My friend **agreed** it was a good idea.

Note: The following expressions change in reported speech.

now = then
today = (on) that day
tomorrow = the day after/the next day
yesterday = the day before

A Listen to the messages on the Johnsons' answering machine and report what the people said.

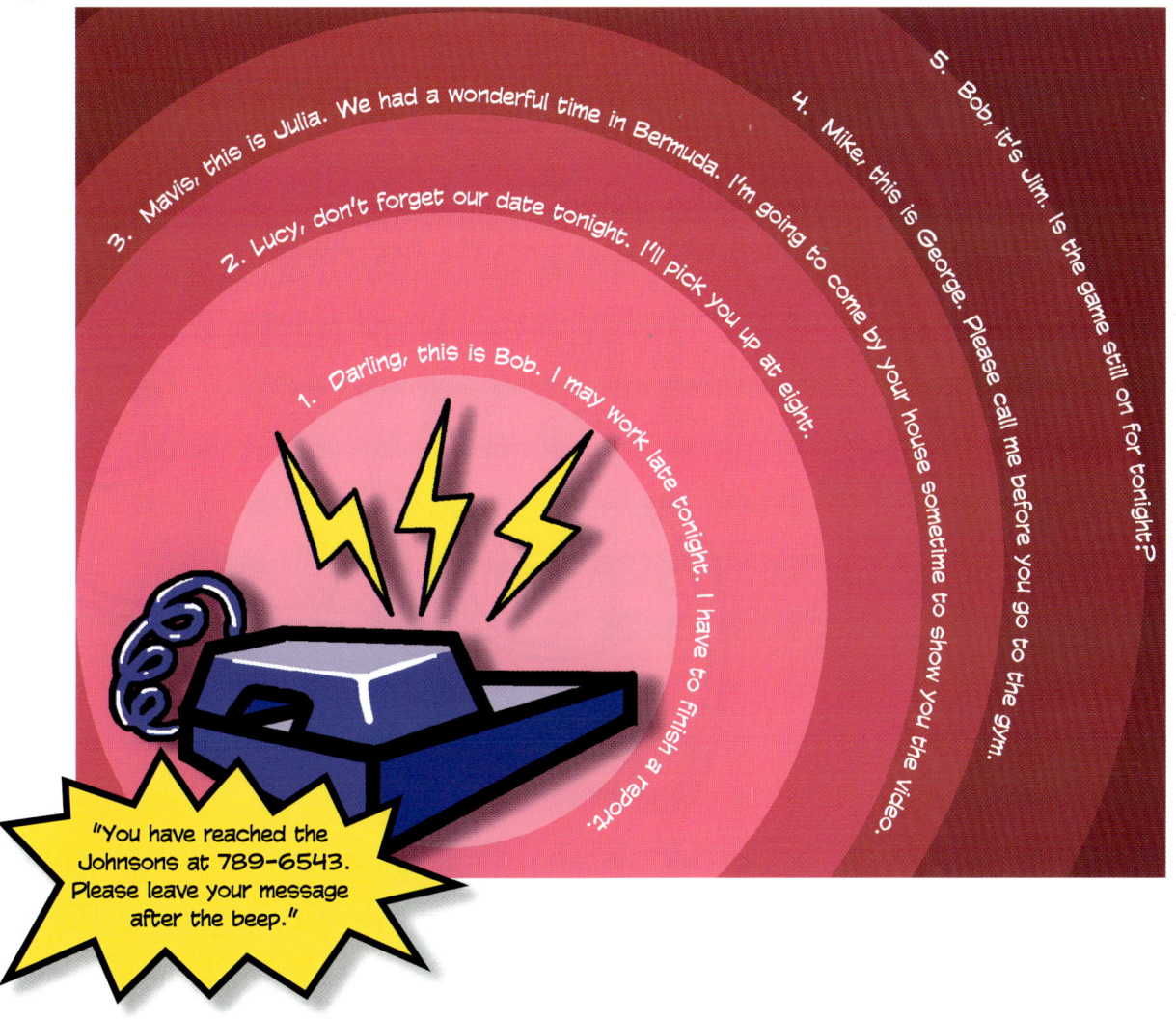

1. Darling, this is Bob. I may work late tonight. I have to finish a report.
2. Lucy, don't forget our date tonight. I'll pick you up at eight.
3. Mavis, this is Julia. We had a wonderful time in Bermuda.
4. Mike, this is George. I'm going to come by your house sometime to show you the video.
5. Bob, it's Jim. Is the game still on for tonight? Please call me before you go to the gym.

"You have reached the Johnsons at 789-6543. Please leave your message after the beep."

B Mike took a message for his sister Lucy.
1. Complete what he wrote down, using the correct form of the verb.
2. Then write the possible telephone conversation between Mike and Derek.

Hi Sis,

That boyfriend of yours (call) _____. He (want to know) _____ where you (be) _____. I (tell) _____ him it (not be) _____ any of his business. He's such an idiot! I said to myself that I (can't) _____ understand why you (go out) _____ with a guy like that. Anyway, he asked me to tell you that he (have) _____ a surprise for you, and that you (should) _____ be ready at eight o'clock tonight. He also suggested that you wear something special, because he (to take) _____ you to a special place. (Ugh!)

Your loving brother,

Mike

4 GRAMMAR TALK

The Telephone Game

Sit in a circle or in rows. The first student whispers something in the ear of the next student. The second student whispers to the third, and so on, until the last student receives the message. The last person to receive the message says it out loud, and the first person says whether it is correct.

5 LISTENING

The presidential candidate made three mistakes, or gaffes, during his speech. Listen and write them down.

1. _____
2. _____
3. _____

6 PRONUNCIATION

Listen and practice.
Each word contains the letter combination *ou*.
Note the different pronunciations.

/ə/	/uw/	/aw/
would	you	our
could		found

7 CHAT TIME

1. Have you ever committed a gaffe? What did you say that you shouldn't have?
2. What was one of the most interesting quotes or sayings that you heard?
3. Are there any sayings that are specific to your country or culture?
4. Have you ever had a telemarketing person call you? What did he/she want to sell? What did he/she say? What did you answer?
5. What messages do you receive or leave on friends' answering machines?
6. Do you and your friends gossip about other people? What is the latest gossip?

8 — CONVERSATION

Lynn: I really think that telemarketing shouldn't be allowed.
Amy: Yes, I agree with you.
Lynn: Yesterday a woman called me up. She said she was from the Dollar Bank, and she asked if she could talk to me for a minute.
Amy: What did she want?
Lynn: She said that someone had given them my name, and that she was calling to offer their services.
Amy: What services?
Lynn: She tried to persuade me to open an account with them. So I told her I already had an account elsewhere, and that I wasn't interested. But she insisted and was very pushy. In the end I lost my patience and told her what I thought of their services.
Amy: Well, I got a call from a man who said he was from a travel agency. This man said I had won a free trip to the Bahamas and that he was calling me to give me the good news.
Lynn: Had you entered a contest or anything like that?
Amy: No. It turned out that the air fare was free, but the amount I'd have to pay for the airport shuttles, hotel, meals, entertainment, and so on would have been more expensive than if I went on my own.

ABOUT THE CONVERSATION
1. What are Lynn and Amy complaining about?
2. What did the woman want?
3. What did Lynn answer?
4. Why did the man call Amy?
5. What would Amy have to do in order to go to the Bahamas?

9 — YOUR TURN

A Role-play the conversation between Lynn and Amy.

B Role-play the conversation that might have taken place between Lynn and the woman or between Amy and the man.

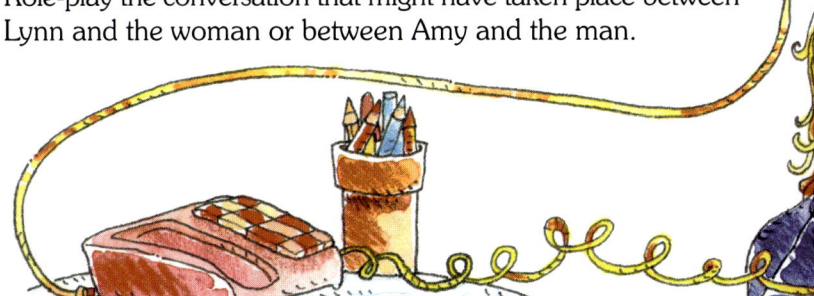

10 READING

BEFORE READING

Do you know any famous quotes? Write them down and compare with a partner.

FAMOUS QUOTES
What they said

"640K ought to be enough for anybody."
Bill Gates in 1981, talking about computer memory (Founder of Microsoft Corp.)

"We don't like their sound, and guitar music is on the way out."
Decca Recording Co., rejecting the Beatles, 1962

"Never let formal education get in the way of your learning."
Mark Twain (Writer)

"It's easy to play any musical instrument: all you have to do is touch the right key at the right time and the instrument will play itself."
Johann Sebastian Bach (Composer)

"Twenty years from now you will be more disappointed by the things that you didn't do than by the ones you did."
Mark Twain (Writer)

"Wise men talk because they have something to say; fools talk because they have to say something."
Plato (Greek Philosopher)

"It is dangerous to be sincere unless you are also stupid."
George Bernard Shaw (Writer)

"When you sit with a nice girl for two hours, you think it's only a minute. But when you sit on a hot stove for a minute, you think it's two hours. That's relativity."
Albert Einstein (Scientist)

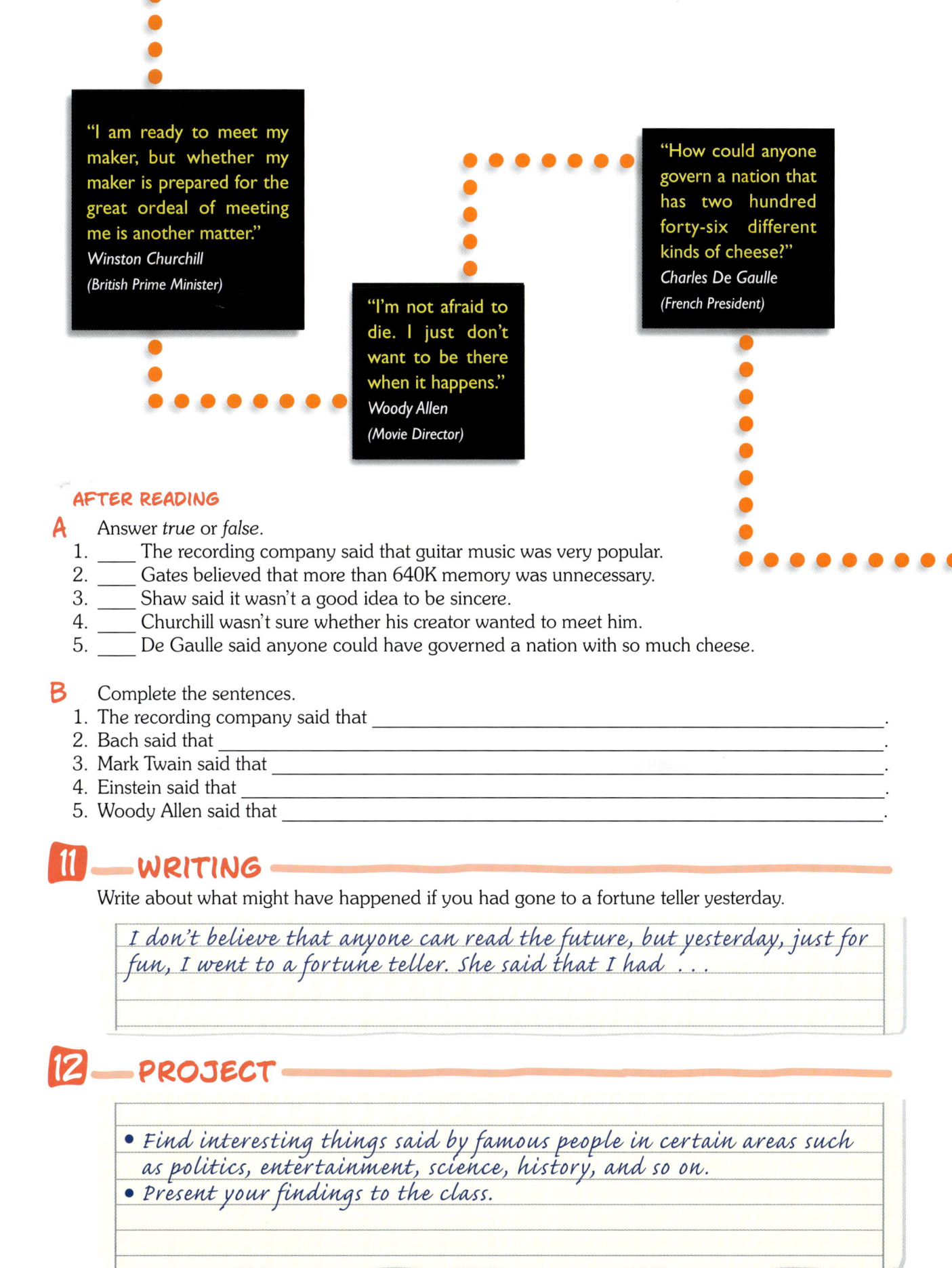

> "I am ready to meet my maker, but whether my maker is prepared for the great ordeal of meeting me is another matter."
> Winston Churchill
> (British Prime Minister)

> "I'm not afraid to die. I just don't want to be there when it happens."
> Woody Allen
> (Movie Director)

> "How could anyone govern a nation that has two hundred forty-six different kinds of cheese?"
> Charles De Gaulle
> (French President)

AFTER READING

A Answer *true* or *false*.
1. ____ The recording company said that guitar music was very popular.
2. ____ Gates believed that more than 640K memory was unnecessary.
3. ____ Shaw said it wasn't a good idea to be sincere.
4. ____ Churchill wasn't sure whether his creator wanted to meet him.
5. ____ De Gaulle said anyone could have governed a nation with so much cheese.

B Complete the sentences.
1. The recording company said that _____.
2. Bach said that _____.
3. Mark Twain said that _____.
4. Einstein said that _____.
5. Woody Allen said that _____.

11 — WRITING

Write about what might have happened if you had gone to a fortune teller yesterday.

> *I don't believe that anyone can read the future, but yesterday, just for fun, I went to a fortune teller. She said that I had . . .*

12 — PROJECT

> - *Find interesting things said by famous people in certain areas such as politics, entertainment, science, history, and so on.*
> - *Present your findings to the class.*

EXPANSION 4

1 — READING

BEFORE READING
1. What do you think the title means?
2. What comes to your mind when people talk about UFOs?

VISITORS FROM BEYOND

One of the most intriguing cases in the history of ufology took place near Roswell, New Mexico, in the U.S. on July 4, 1947. A strange object which had been detected on the radar for three days suddenly disappeared. The amazing speed and erratic motion indicated that it couldn't have been a plane or a meteorite. Several people in the Roswell area said that they had witnessed the crash: William Mac Brasel as well as others had heard a tremendous explosion; William Woody and his father had seen a flaming object fall to earth; and Jim Ragsdale and Trudy Truelove had observed a bright light crash near their campsite.

A special retrieval team arrived from Washington and located the crashed craft. They took the names of all the civilians on the site, and they escorted them away. The area was cleaned and secured within five or six hours, and five bodies were removed. Melvin Brown, who was one of the guards in the truck transporting the bodies, claims that they were small with large heads and that their skin was an orange-yellow color.

Mac Brasel found some strange debris in his field and drove into Roswell to show it to the sheriff, who in turn informed the military. The military sent Jesse A. Marcel and Captain Sheridan Cavitt to investigate. Neither of them had ever seen anything like it. The foil-like substance would not burn or scratch, and when held in the hand, it felt weightless. If several pieces of the substance were crumpled into a ball, they would return to their original shape when released. Marcel loaded as much of the material as he could into his car and took it back with him to show to his superiors.

Rumors started spreading around that a flying saucer had been discovered, and the Air Force in Fort Worth confirmed the story. Within a couple of hours the base was flooded with calls from around the world. A press conference was arranged, but the remains of the flying saucer that Marcel had brought back with him were gone and had been replaced with bits from an old weather balloon. Marcel was ordered to be photographed with the balloon debris and not to say anything about it. General Ramey explained that the men at Roswell had made a mistake, and the story died down.

There have been many hoaxes associated with this case, including the infamous "Alien Autopsy Video." Many interesting books have been written about what happened, or might have happened, at Roswell. However, forty years later, the U.S. government finally admitted that the "weather balloon" story had indeed been a cover-up.

AFTER READING

A Answer about the text.
1. Why couldn't the object have been a plane or meteorite?
2. What did the witnesses say about the object?
3. What did Brown say about the incident?
4. Had Marcel ever seen a similar substance before?
5. What explanation did the military give about the Roswell incident?

B Find other words in the text that mean
1. an unidentified flying object (UFO)
2. remains or fragments
3. position or place; location
4. a made-up story

DISCUSSION

1. What do you think might have happened/could have happened at Roswell?
2. What would you have done if you had been Mac Brasel or Marcel?
3. Do you believe there is intelligent life in other galaxies?
   Mark your reasons under the corresponding column. Discuss with your classmates.

For	Against

2 — WRITING

Imagine you interviewed the people who witnessed the Roswell incident.
Write the dialog you had with them.

3 — ACTIVITIES

A What would you have done or said in the following situations?

"I have a reservation."

"Sorry, sir. The flight is overbooked."

B Imagine you make contact with extraterrestrial beings. What questions would you ask them?

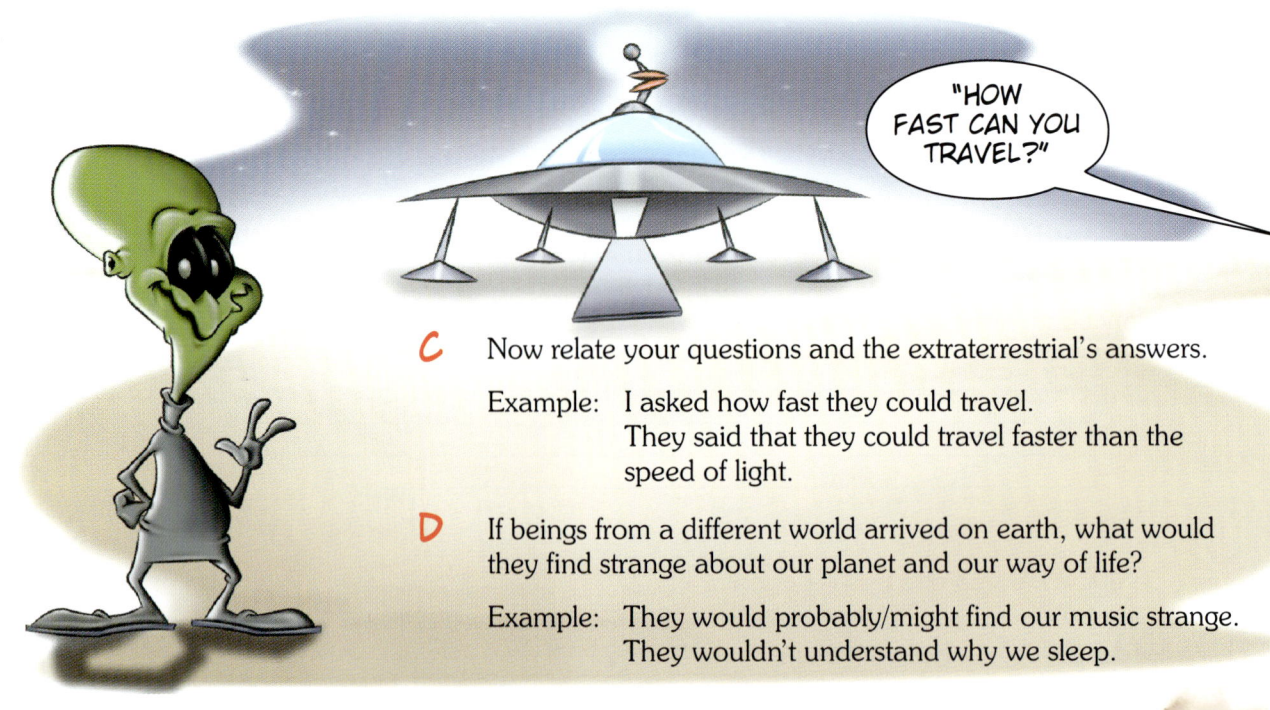

"HOW FAST CAN YOU TRAVEL?"

C Now relate your questions and the extraterrestrial's answers.

Example: I asked how fast they could travel.
They said that they could travel faster than the speed of light.

D If beings from a different world arrived on earth, what would they find strange about our planet and our way of life?

Example: They would probably/might find our music strange.
They wouldn't understand why we sleep.

E   Read about the strange house built by Sarah Pardee Winchester.
Complete the text with the correct form of each verb in parentheses.

THE WINCHESTER HOUSE

In 1862, Sarah Pardee (marry) _____ William Wirt Winchester. William was the son of the inventor and maker of the famous Winchester rifles. When her husband (die) _____, a medium in Boston told Sarah that his death (be caused) _____ by the spirits of the thousands who (be shot) _____ by Winchester rifles. He also told her that the only way to escape the evil spirits was to build a house and (increase) _____ its size constantly. Sarah (move) _____ to an eighteen-bedroom house in San Jose, California, and in six months she (have) _____ another eighteen rooms (build) _____ onto the house. She (continue) _____ to add extra rooms for the next thirty-eight years. The medium said the plans (be give) _____ to her by the spirits, and the designs were very strange indeed. Some stairs (lead) _____ to the ceiling, other rooms had no floors, and so forth. When Sarah Pardee (pass away) _____ in 1922, at the age of eighty-five, she (build) _____ a total of one hundred sixty rooms.

4 — TALK ABOUT IT

1. Do you believe in ghosts and spirits?
   Have you ever heard or read about people who have had contact with them?
2. What would you do if strange incidents started happening in your house?

Vocabulary

1 BACKGROUNDS

VOCABULARY

Nouns			Verbs	Adverbs	Adjectives
accent	ferryboat	nation	direct	deep down	average
amateur	folks	native	express	extremely	fair
ancestor	freckles	performance	fail	pretty	fluent
background	freedom	prosperity	immigrate	quite	good-looking
compartment	generation	public appearance	major	rather	native
degree	great-grandfather	public relations	manage	somewhat	outgoing
descent	immigrant	railroad	question		prosperous
dorm	impression	roots	rehearse		reserved
dramatic arts	keyboard	slim	trace		smelly
ethnic	medical exam	village	welcome		sociable

EXPRESSIONS

become known	keep in touch
have something in common	right away

2 CAREERS

VOCABULARY

Nouns		
application	flavor	pearl
archeologist	gossip column	press
award	gourmet	qualifications
blend	graduate	resume
blueprint	intern	ruins
buried	internship	shares
career	issue	shell
challenge	knowledge	skill
construction	lava	slogan
crack	liquid	spot
dig	lodging	step
environment	media	stockbroker
equipment	merchant	substance
fee	opportunity	supply
fitness	oyster	volcano

Verbs		
advertise	investigate	purchase
apply	involve	require
combine	place	select
cultivate	pour	work out
find out	produce	
hire	provide	

Adjectives	
alert	fascinating
ceramic	further
critical	private
discreet	smooth
experienced	various

EXPRESSIONS

come up with something	good at something
depend on	have a good sense of

3 WHAT WILL BE WILL BE

VOCABULARY

Nouns		Verbs		Adjectives	Adverbs
automobile	network	burst	mend	dear	automatically
character	novel	consider	program	gas-powered	precisely
composer	pipe	exist	recognize	high-powered	shortly
cottage	plumber	feed	retire	high-speed	
depth	robot	figure out	wonder	household	**Prepositions**
fingerprint	rocket	fill up			around
fire extinguisher	skyscraper	influence			along (with)
fireside	submarine	lock			
fuse	system				
gadget	weed				
life expectancy	whale				
monitor					

EXPRESSIONS

be able to afford	do the cleaning/gardening/ironing/washing	scrimp and save
be handy	drop a line	waste away
by the end of	go for a ride	

4 ONLY THE BEST

VOCABULARY

Nouns		Verbs	Adjectives		Adverbs
accessories	hot-dog stand	conquer	amazing	mysterious	comfortably
ad	jar	design	ancient	natural	extravagantly
aroma	machinery	develop	available	precious	
attention	odor	disappear	compact	resistant	**Preposition**
banquet	pedal	experience	drive-in	significant	throughout
blacksmith	rank	imply	dumb	sophisticated	
bumper	ruler	introduce	economical	special	
chain	safety feature	launch	fashionable	tiny	
commercial	scent	pack	homemade	trusted	
concept	spice	prove	inexpensive	versatile	
effect	trunk	put through	luxury		
engine	variety	reach			
fragrance	wood	replace			
herb		spring up			

EXPRESSIONS

according to . . .	I bet . . .	made by/of
ever since	look/smell/sound/taste like	the (bigger) the . . . , the (better) the . . .

5 DID YOU HURT YOURSELF?

VOCABULARY

Nouns		
adolescent	hip	roast
ankle	industry	sidewalk
antiseptic	injury	slides
awning	legend	stitch
can opener	meteorite	swings
concrete	mitts	thunderstorm
curb	monkey bars	tricycle
fatality	pacifier	vehicle
forehead	playground	windowsill
fracture	rate	wrist

Verbs	
approach	land
blow	lean
burn	occur
cut	rush
dive	slip
grab	splash
hurt	sprain
injure	survive

Adjectives
desperate
minor
mischievous
poisonous
slippery

Adverbs
instantly
likely

Conjunction
in case

EXPRESSIONS

be aware	do something oneself	lose one's balance
be run over	fall out of (a window)	senior citizen
be sound asleep	get a shock	use with care
be struck by lightning	hit/fall face first	
be up to something	keep out of reach	

6 TAKE MY ADVICE

VOCABULARY

Nouns	
alcohol	instinct
anorexia	karate
appetite	mood
condition	morals
dating	possession
divorce	reason
drug	relationship
excuse	respect
feelings	site
hermit	tobacco
honesty	values

Verbs	
affect	last
avoid	let
cheat	respect
control	tolerate
determine	trust
encourage	

Adverbs	
downhill	suddenly
simply	unsafe

Adjectives	
abusive	old-fashioned
common	physical
desirable	self-defense
emotional	slim
illegal	verbal
jealous	warning

Conjunctions
in order to
therefore

EXPRESSIONS

be under stress	get straight As	make a choice	show off
break up	have one's way	make the team	stay away from something
feel good about oneself	keep fit	peer pressure	take up a sport
feel sorry for oneself	keep one's principles	put something off	turn something down
gain weight	keep one's weight down	reach one's goal	turn to someone
get along with	lose weight	refer to	

7 DEAR FRIENDS

VOCABULARY

Nouns
bowling alley
code
column
combination
conference
dialect
focus
method
possibility
revolution
speech
Stone Age
tone
tower

Verbs
alternate
apologize
attend
deliver
establish
excuse
expand
freeze
identify
increase
indicate
relate
simulate
transmit
view

Adjectives
absent
distant
powerful
remote
successful
unable
widespread

Adverbs
almost
nowadays

Conjunctions
although
as soon as
despite
in spite of

EXPRESSIONS

be used to
get engaged
look forward to
set up a time
take place
That's a shame!
will/won't be able to make it
yours sincerely
yours truly

8 WISHFUL THINKING

VOCABULARY

Nouns
amount
animal skin
barley
canoe
castaway
cave
charity
companion
creature
crew
desire
expectation
extraterrestrial
figure
frustration
game show
goat
grain
guillotine
gun
jackpot
journal
lottery
raisins
sack
shipwreck
shore
solitude
stock market
storm
supplies
survivor
tools
wish

Verbs
anchor
discover
divide
drown
dry
invest
store
succeed
vary
wreck

Adjectives
clay
desert
fabulous
frightening
historical
lonely
loyal
protected
real-life
sole
uninhabited

Adverbs
aboard
eventually
exactly
unexpectedly

EXPRESSIONS

be crazy
be tossed up
close encounter
end up
lack of something
the whole year round

117

9 COMPLAINTS, COMPLAINTS

VOCABULARY

Nouns
awareness	dent	landlord	Realtor	sleeve
brand	doorknob	lane	receipt	theory
coincidence	DVD player	law	refund	thermostat
complaint	faucet	manual	rights	waist
consumer	floorboard	memory	seam	warranty
creation	housing	popcorn	season	windowpane
dealer	label	probability	service	windshield

Adjectives
baggy	leaky
chipped	loose
cracked	pushy
damaged	scratched
faded	sewn
filthy	similar
fuzzy	torn
incorrect	tricky

Verbs
adjust	drip	gather	pop	split
blame	exchange	influence	product	stain
button	expect	occur	question	tend
calculate	fix	offer	return	tie
dispute				

Adverbs
closely	readily
fortunately	unfortunately
necessarily	

EXPRESSIONS
- all set to do something
- be in style
- be satisfied
- break down
- finance charge
- get one's money back
- get/have something done
- good/bad credit record
- have one's car serviced
- run out of something
- sound like

10 I WONDER WHAT HAPPENED

VOCABULARY

Nouns
acre	darkness	melon
altitude	desert	object
approach	detective	parking lot
army	extinction	photosynthesis
asteroid	force	region
atmosphere	foundation	shock wave
cannonball	headquarters	solar system
crane	high-rise	spacecraft
crater	impact	technology
damage	insurance	weapon

Verbs
bend
circulate
cover
demolish
destroy
devastate
explode
own
penetrate
persist
prevent
strike

Adjectives
accepted
horrible
huge
negligible
nuclear
seaside

Adverbs
approximately
harmlessly
immediately
nearby
whenever
wherever

Pronouns
whatever
whoever

EXPRESSIONS
- be concerned
- blow up something
- brand new
- check out something
- have a look
- knock over
- make room for something
- over here/there
- put up something
- snap off
- wipe out

11 IF I'D ONLY KNOWN

VOCABULARY

Nouns
boss
briefcase
cab
candidate
destination
doubt
employee
flat
master
master's degree
position
regret
responsibility
royalty
sweetheart

Verbs
argue
cater
fight
notice
regret
reward
share
treat
wish

Adjectives
confused
financial
grateful
immature
second-hand
stable

Adverb
differently

EXPRESSIONS

all over again
all the way
as far as
be mad at someone
down payment
go one's own way
have one's mind set
If only I had . . .
make trouble
wait on tables

12 WHAT THEY SAID

VOCABULARY

Nouns
amount
contest
entertainment
fool
inhabitant
ordeal
proof
quote
relativity
shuttle
stove
telemarketing
X-ray

Verbs
bother
examine
govern
insist
persuade
touch
X-ray

Adjectives
positive
sincere

Adverb
elsewhere

EXPRESSIONS

be allowed
be on its way out
be prepared
call someone up
lose one's patience
make contact

119

EXPANSION 1

VOCABULARY

Nouns
bone	makeup	remains
cheek	nomad	ritual
decoration	ochre	scar
dot	ore	surface
eyelid	pattern	tattoo
heritage	pigment	tradition
iron	powder	trend

Verbs
- decorate
- dye
- grind
- mark
- preserve
- rub
- trace

Adjectives
- elaborate
- facial
- indigenous
- prehistoric

EXPRESSIONS
- belong to
- date back

EXPANSION 2

VOCABULARY

Nouns
ability	expert	pressure
adolescence	fitness	preteen
adulthood	flexibility	resort
attitude	generation	response
audience	insomnia	self-esteem
behavior	memory	spa
bulimia	moodiness	stress
childhood	nutritionist	symptom
concentration	outlook	technique
court	peer	tip
deadline	perception	villa
demand	preoccupation	youngster

Verbs
- accomplish
- achieve
- adjust
- cease
- dedicate
- emerge
- increase
- necessary
- unnecessary

Adjectives
- carefree
- constant
- exquisite
- gourmet
- qualified
- similar
- tremendous
- unique

Adverbs
- definitely
- indoor

EXPRESSIONS
- a step at a time
- be surrounded by
- do well
- eating/sleeping disorder
- loss of appetite
- no charge
- peace of mind

EXPANSION 3

VOCABULARY

Nouns
base, ladder, batter, league, bladder, legend, bounce, opponent, caribou, peach, civilization, pitch, core, settler, cricket, strike, home plate, umpire, innovation

Verbs
contain, create, defeat, devise, fill, project, score, spread

Adjectives
bouncy, brave, Colonial, official, rough, rubber, vertical, wooden

Adverbs
apart, indoors, slightly

Prepositions
opposite, throughout

EXPRESSIONS

barehanded
be given credit for something
for instance
made up of
put together
swing at something

EXPANSION 4

VOCABULARY

Nouns
alien, hoax, campsite, medium, ceiling, radar, debris, remains, explosion, rifle, flying saucer, spirit, foil, superior, guard

Verbs
admit, observe, claim, remove, confirm, replace, crumple, scratch, detect, secure, escort, transport, indicate, witness, investigate

Adjectives
flaming, infamous, intriguing, tremendous, weightless

Preposition
beyond

EXPRESSIONS

a cover-up
be flooded
die down
take place